PLEASE STOP SAYING THAT!

An irreverent look at clichés and buzzwords from American business, journalism, pop culture, religion, social media and sports

STEPHEN H. PROVOST

Cover artwork: Public domain images
Cover concept and design: Stephen H. Provost
All interior images are in the public domain.

Dragon Crown Books 2018

ISBN-13: 978-1-7320632-9-7

Please Stop Saying That!

CONTENTS

DEDICATION

To all the copy editors who worked so hard to make newspapers legible and television news watchable — many of whom lost their jobs despite that hard work.

ACKNOWLEDGEMENTS

A number of people suggested entries that ultimately made it into this book. Among them: Amber Andrade, Mary Ann Back, Martina Crews, VicToria Freudiger, Rachel Griffin, Bailey Hunter, Ruth Kehler, Caroline Jackson, Michele Miller, Andrew Milne, Nora B. Peevy, Samaire Provost, Mark Rainey, Ronda Thompson, Linda Tooch, Terri VanKuipers, Maureen Duffy Walker and Lynn Werner.

Introduction

Once upon a time, I was promoted to copy desk chief at a midsize daily newspaper in Central California, and one of my first duties was to create a local stylebook. What I enjoyed most about this task was identifying the kind of jargon, clichés and associated silliness I didn't want to see in the newspaper.

Things like, "The car drove to the 3000 block of Birch Street." (Cars don't drive. People drive them.) Or the fire was "fully involved." (Involved with what? Its "hot" significant other? Watching *Monday Night Football*? Playing *Pokemon Go*?)

In addition to such odd constructions, a slew of words and phrases threatened to make their way into the pages of the newspaper — and we on the copy desk were determined to stop them. Our top editors called us "the last line of defense"; they even created an award with that title.

This work is the bastard stepchild of that project. Consider it your last line of defense against the banal inanities that assault your ears on a daily basis. Its purpose is to poke fun at them, which is really all most of them are good for: poking fun at. The entries fall into several categories, among them:

• Terms only serious sports fans would know, often used by sportscasters who aren't too sure how to use them themselves.

• Business propaganda aimed at getting the most work out of employees for the least amount of money while offering the bare minimum in job security.

• Pop culture terms likely to leave those of us over a certain age scratching their heads.

• Terms used in religious gatherings to make people feel closer to God while simultaneously getting them emotionally hyped up or, alternatively, putting them to sleep.

• B.S. used in ads to make you buy things.

• B.S. used by politicians to make you buy more B.S.

• B.S. used by lobbyists, political activists and others that encourages you to buy the B.S. used by politicians, thereby exposing you to further B.S.

• Hyperbole employed by cable news talking heads designed to get you to tune in, veg out and watch the network's commercials. Similar efforts by online journalists that amount to a continual, insistent whine of "CLICK ON ME! CLICK ON ME!" (For more on this, see my book *Media Meltdown*.)

This book pokes fun at the words people use in

discussing politics, religion, sports and other sensitive subjects. If you're allergic to sarcasm about such sacred cows, please get yourself inoculated before going any further, because chances are, this book will poke fun at something you're in the habit of saying when talking about these subjects. Don't take it personally. I've uttered many of these words and phrases myself, and I've belonged (or still belong) to groups in the habit of using them, so I'm making fun of myself and my peer groups as much as I am anyone else.

This is by no means an exhaustive list: There are about 300 entries, not the 470,000 in Merriam-Webster. If I'm missing something important, I might just have to come out with a second edition, but I'm not going to sweat it, and you shouldn't, either. It's just a book, but one that I hope you'll have fun reading.

Notes:

- Underlined text refers to other entries within this work.
- I've included parts of speech in parentheses for clarification, as follows: (abbr.)-abbreviation, (acr.)-acronym, (adj.)-adjective, (adv.)-adverb, (conj.)-conjunction, (decl.)-declaration, (intj.)-interjection, (n.)-noun, (prep.)-preposition/prepositional phrase, (qstn.)-question, (suff.)-suffix, (v.)-verb. For phrases, the dominant part of speech is used.

The List

Absolutely! (intj.)

Who uses it – Riders of bandwagons. Guests on news talk shows who have been fed leading questions by hosts desperately searching for someone else to give weight to their opinions.

What it means – "I agree with you, one hundred percent. I wish I'd said that myself! In fact, I would have said it myself if you hadn't beat me to it. You took the words right out of my mouth. We must be kindred spirits. Soul mates. You must be omniscient – because you agree with me!"

What it sounds like – You're brown-nosing.

Accessory (n.)

Who uses it – Police and lawyers.

What it means – Someone who didn't commit a crime directly but who nonetheless violated the law by helping someone else do so. Someone who aids and abets.

What it sounds like – A handbag. "Accessory after the fact"? That would be a secondhand handbag.

Acid test (n.)

Who uses it – Journalists who want to sound edgy; lazy writers.

What it means – A test that will conclusively prove whether or not something's worth a shit.

What it used to mean – The use of acid by miners to distinguish between gold and other metals during the California Gold Rush.

What it sounds like – A student at Berkeley taking his finals on LSD. That's the drug that makes you see things like a T-rex charging at you on the freeway, a singing hippopotamus or the ghost of Gandhi brushing his teeth in your water closet. (That's a European term for bathroom; I only used it because I wanted an excuse to do so.) LSD should not be confused with LDS, a religious belief that makes you wear weird underpants and promises to crown you absolute ruler of your very own planet after you die. Come to think of it, that's pretty trippy, too.

Across the aisle (prep.)

Who uses it – Politicians pretending they respect, and are at least willing to listen to positions taken by the opposition party (aka "The Devil," "Satan" and "He Who Must Not Be Named").

What it means – A rumored, quite possibly mythical place where everyone holds hands, roasts marshmallows, sings Kumbaya and cosponsors legislation for the common good. It's been so long since anyone's been there that no one knows the way ... or if it even exists. Politicians on each side tell their respective "bases" during primary season that it's another name for hell. Then, during the general election, they often describe it as Shangri-La and portray themselves as the only ones equipped to lead the country there.

What it used to mean – A real, viable political option.

What it sounds like – Where the Cap'n Crunch is when you can't find it at the Super Walmart.

Action plan (n.)

Who uses it – An executive groping for a "new approach" to set him apart from a fired predecessor.

What it means – I'm not sure. It's pretty hard to plan to do nothing, which would be the alternative. I mean, really nothing at all. Even if you're sleeping or meditating, you're doing *something*. If you plan to sit around staring at your navel or lie in bed listening to crickets chirp, those actions might not be world-changing, but they're still actions. I suspect the point of calling something an "action" plan is to make it sound dynamic, even though it's meaningless unless you're trying to contrast it with someone who's comatose. Or dead.

What it used to mean – I'm convinced that, prior to the 20th century, no one would have been stupid enough to use this phrase.

Aid and abet (v.)

Who uses it – Police and lawyers who like to emphasize how serious something is through repetition ("abet" is just another word for "aid.")

What it means – Something an accessory (not a handbag) does.

What it sounds like – Something that might get you beaten up if you're standing behind one poker player and signaling another player at the table: aid in a bet.

Alt-right (adj., n.)

Who uses it – Journalists who don't want to come off as too judgmental by labeling people racist pigs.

What it means – Xenophobic and racist, with a thinly veiled desire to take over the known universe. The KKK meets Darth Sidius. A euphemism to describe white supremacists who want to pass themselves off as mainstream conservatives, or as a legitimate alternative to them.

What it sounds like – Pathetic, dangerous and entirely unacceptable fascist bullshit. Also: A keyboard command.

Amen! (intj.)

Who uses it – Churchgoers and people who want to sound like churchgoers because they think it sounds hip or enhances their credibility (the righteous and the self-righteous, who are sometimes one and the same).

What it means – The same thing as "Absolutely!" but with a religious connotation that (supposedly) lends it more gravitas, especially when followed by the term "brother" or "sister." Traditionally uttered at the end of a prayer, its actual meaning is "so be it" or – to quote Patrick

Stewart as Jean-Luc Picard – "make it so." Ahead, warp factor six.

What it sounds like – You forgot to say a prayer and skipped to the end. Learn some patience!

And-one (n., intj.)

Who uses it – Basketball announcers.

What it means – A foul shot after a made basket that gives the player an opportunity to make a three- or four-point play. It can be used as a declarative statement or as a noun, referring to "an and-one," which makes it sound even more awkward to anyone who's not a sports fan. But sports fans themselves are a different breed. They're renowned for accepting goofy jargon that would evoke guffaws from the rest of the world as though it were solemn gospel truth just because it was intoned by a color commentator or someone who claims to be versed in the sacred tongue of analytics.

What it sounds like – Antoine.

Anti-hero (n.)

Who uses it – Readers and critics of graphic novels

or the blockbuster movies based on them.

What it means – A vigilante or mercenary, which is supposedly cool because it's in a comic book even though such people get arrested in the real world. A despicable character who qualifies as the protagonist because, on just one occasion, when it matters most, he succeeds in *not* acting like the sonofabitch he really is. Or in acting that way but accomplishing something noble in spite of it. Or because of it.

What it sounds like – A villain.

Apprehend (v.)

Who uses it – Police and journalists who quote them without realizing that, when they do, they sound like police officers themselves.

What it means – The person was arrested. Whether or not the person was apprehensive about being arrested before it happened is irrelevant. Whether or not the person apprehended (was aware of) what was happening at the time is also irrelevant. Either way, the person was still arrested.

What it sounds like – Something you'd hear on a police scanner, or an old episode of *Adam-12* or *Dragnet.*

Asking for a friend (decl.)

Who uses it – Social media users.

What it means – "I have an embarrassing problem that I don't want to admit I'm dealing with, but I don't know the answer and I need some advice, so I'll pretend to be asking about it on behalf of some nameless friend." But this phrase has been used so often, it has become a joke, a way of saying, "I know this is incredibly transparent and everyone who reads this will realize it applies to me, but maybe being cute about it will take the edge off. Wink, wink. Nudge, nudge. Say no more."

What it sounds like – You've been spending too much time on social media.

At the end of the day (prep.)

Who uses it – Cable news hosts who need to summarize what's been said because they're up against a commercial break; writers who don't know how to create an elegant transition between an argument and a conclusion.

What it means – "When all is said and done" or "in the final analysis," two equally annoying phrases that seem to have been largely supplanted by this one, for no apparent reason other than the Law of Ubiquitous Irritation. This principle states plainly that if one badly overused, vacant expression falls into disuse, another must inevitably arise to take its place, piling additional syllables onto sentences that would have been clearer without them.

What it used to mean – A period in the normal 23-hour, 56-minute cycle during which the sun appears to be just above, resting on or just below the horizon, commonly known as "sunset" or "twilight." Alternatively: the time at which the clock strikes midnight and everyone's car turns back into a pumpkin.

Authorities (n.)

Who uses it – Reporters who need someone else to say something's important but know they can't say it on their own and don't want to be blasted for using the even vaguer "inside sources" or "sources with knowledge of this matter."

What it means – In journalism, a stock term that's used to identify important people without really identifying them. It tells readers/viewers nothing about *who* these nameless authorities are, *what* they're authorities on or *why* they're qualified to be authorities in the first place. They might be police officers, scientists, a bubble-gum-blowing expert from Duluth, or none of the above. An alternative to the equally vague and useless phrase, "the powers that be."

What it sounds like – Pretty damned presumptuous. Not to mention lazy. Cowardly. Oh, and condescending.

Backslide (v.)

Who uses it – Preachers who don't want you to do this, because you might wind up in hell or, worse, stop attending Sunday services and paying your tithes.

What it means – Give in to temptation or, worse, become what used to be known as an apostate. This means someone who actively renounces a religious belief and is by no means to be confused with an apostle ... although even apostles can become apostates (prime examples: Peter when the cock crowed and Judas in exchange for thirty pieces of silver). The religious equivalent to an alcoholic falling off the wagon.

What it sounds like – Going down a waterslide on

your back, which is a lot less scary than going down on your stomach face-first. Now *that* takes faith!

Bae (n.)

Who uses it – People who want to sound like they're up to date on pop culture, even though they're at least a decade behind the times.

What it means – A significant other.

What it used to mean – The sound a bleating lamb makes, which is kind of like the sound people make when they say this. Spelled differently, a brown horse with a black mane that makes a very different kind of sound, called a "neigh," which rhymes with "bae" and is just about as meaningful (more so, come to think about it, because whenever anyone uses this word, I want to respond by saying "nay").

What it used to mean, too – A homonym for a body of water, as in Green Bay or Hudson Bay or San Francisco Bay, all of which are far more pleasant to look at than "bae" is to hear.

Bearish (adj.)

Who uses it – Investors who don't like the word "pessimistic."

What it means – Pessimistic; the opposite of "bullish," presumably because bulls charge ahead recklessly and bears retreat into their caves for the winter. The bear market, incidentally, is not a place to buy grizzlies and pandas. It's a place where people screw up your retirement to selling off pieces of paper, meaning you can't go into hibernation and have to keep working until you're an old, grizzled shell of a person and it's no longer bearable.

What it sounds like – You've just got to grin and bear it.

Beat a dead horse (v.)

Who uses it – People tired of listening to know-it-all windbags push ideas that are never going to go anywhere. Most common context: business meetings, political debates.

What it means – Staying on the same subject even though you've already devoted a lot of time to it without making any headway.

What it sounds like – If anyone bothered to

visualize what this means, I'm convinced people would stop saying it. The phrase is so sadistic that it should be reported to the SPCA.

Believer (n.)

Who uses it – Protestant Christians, particularly those who attend evangelical, Pentecostal and/or charismatic churches.

What it means – Another Christian. Usually another Protestant Christian. Most commonly another evangelical Protestant Christian and preferably a baptized, spirit-filled, Bible-believing Protestant Christian from the same denomination, same church and same pew.

What it sounds like – Someone who believes something. Anything. Which would include every member of the human race. We're all God's children, after all.

Best practices (n.)

Who uses it – Human resources drones.

What it means – "You need to read this dense, boring policy manual because it's company policy, which is so much more virtuous than anything you dumbass workers might come up with if you consulted your own consciences."

What it sounds like – Some purposely vague B.S. that is an improvement on "better practices" and infinitely superior to "worst practices."

BFF (abbr., n.)

Who uses it – People trying to establish a sense of permanence in their relationships.

What it means – Best friends forever.

What it sounds like – The kind of person who could become a stalker if you have a falling out. Forever is a very long time. One question: If you are "kind of" a BFF, does that make you BFF-y, and does that, in turn, make you a vampire slayer?

Bite me (v.)

Who uses it – The generation before the one that used "talk to the hand."

What it means – F.U., more politely. Something you don't want to say to Fido if you find out he has rabies.

What it sounds like – An invitation to a vampire.

Bleeding heart (n., adj.)

Who uses it – People who think compassion is a sign of weakness; often a compound modifier used before "liberal."

What it means – "You want a living wage? Affordable health care? Brownie points for people who help little old ladies across the street and adopt animals from the shelter? Grow a pair! Empathy is for wimps. If you haven't figured out that nice guys finish last, you deserve to be taken advantage of. By us."

What it sounds like – Someone had better call an ambulance.

Bless your heart (intj.)

Who uses it – People who don't want to do that.

What it means – "You're a real idiot." Often uttered in a condescending tone and with an accent. Sarcastic in the same way as any rhetorical question that begins with "Aren't you just ...?" (the cat's meow, a real genius, etc.) The implied answer being "hell no!" A strong candidate to become an entry in the ever-expanding Orwellian dictionary of doublespeak.

What it used to mean – Just what it says. In the same way that "bad" used to mean "bad," before it became an expression to signify the exact opposite and the title of Michael Jackson's multiplatinum follow-up to *Thriller*. Whether that album was "bad" in the colloquial sense or truly bad depends on your taste in music.

Blessed be (intj.)

Who uses it – Pagans, Wiccans, and members of Earth-based spiritual traditions.

What it means – The same thing as "God bless" means for Christians, but not the same thing as "bless your heart."

What it sounds like – Yoda's way of saying "be blessed." A fortunate bee.

Blog (n.)

Who uses it – Internet users.

What it means – A shortened form of the term "weblog," which itself is a combination of "web" and "log." This is a truly special term: Is there any other word that has been created by taking the last letter of the prefix and slapping it onto the suffix? Not that I know of. And it happened in such a short period of time. "Weblog" was born in the 1990s and, within just a few years, it had become archaic. No one says "weblog" anymore, because everyone is too lazy to utter two whole syllables. But take heart: Apparently this term will not survive into the 23rd century, by which time starship captains will have reverted to the more primitive term, expressed as part of the introductory phrase, "captain's log, star date ..."

What it sounds like – A bodily function. A nebulous mass found in a fallen tree.

Bombshell (n.)

Who uses it – TV news anchors trying to justify calling something "breaking news." Calling it a bombshell makes it sound a lot more important and unexpected than it really is.

What it means – "Wow! Listen to this! No one would have ever expected *this* to happen. But because we're telling you about it, we're very, very connected and very, very, very important!"

What it used to mean – A shell encasing a powerful explosive device, often dropped from an airplane.

Alternatively: Marilyn Monroe or Jean Harlowe or Mae West or Jayne Mansfield.

Boots on the ground (n.)

Who uses it – Politicians who got out of serving in the military by claiming they had bone spurs or hangnails, and who have never worn boots because such footwear isn't allowed on the golf course.

What it means – Sending people into a dangerous situation while you sit back in your "situation room" or corporate suite and smoke a stogie. Similar to phrases such as trench warfare and guerrilla (not gorilla) warfare. Translation: "We want to sound like we're willing to get our hands dirty, even though we're corporate executives with corner suites, guaranteed pensions and parachute clauses in our contracts" (or, alternatively, "politicians who will make six figures on book deals and speaking tours after we've done our time in Washington").

What it sounds like – Someone watched *Rambo* and *Saving Private Ryan* one too many times.

Boys will be boys (decl.)

Who uses it – Idiots who want to excuse bad

behavior based on a person's "outie" genitalia.

What it means – "Johnny pulled Mary's hair, spit in the cafeteria food, beat up the neighbor kid and stole his lunch money. It's all OK. He's got a penis. Never mind the fact that he's 45 years old."

What it sounds like – Something you might hear from an irresponsible parent or a politician seeking to excuse "minor indiscretions" like driving drunk, getting into bar fights, hiring prostitutes or cheating on their taxes.

Breaking news (n.)

Who uses it – Cable news stations and online news sites competing for an increasingly fragmented audience so they can charge advertisers as much as possible for largely ineffective exposure.

What it means – "We want you to watch our TV station or click on our website, so we're going to tell you something important just happened! Please try to ignore the fact that we apply this label to anything that happened over the past 48 hours, whether it involves a nuclear bomb being dropped or your neighbor Helga's cat being rescued from a jade bush."

What it used to mean – President Kennedy has just been assassinated. A man just set foot on the moon.

Terrorists just flew planes into skyscrapers. The Cubs won the World Series. That sort of thing.

Brainstorm (n.)

Who uses it – People, particularly in business, who are out of ideas.

What it means – A bunch of people who can't come up with a reasonable approach to a problem get together and waste a lot of time tossing out silly, unworkable ideas. They mutually agree not to laugh about any of these while they're together, responding to each with solemn nods and furrowed brows. Then they go home and tell their significant others all about it: "You'll never believe the idiotic idea Joe came up with!"

What it sounds like – Something that goes on inside the head of Frankenstein's monster just as the lightning strikes.

Broken record (n.)

Who uses it – Members of the Humane Society who want to get someone to stop talking but who can't, for ethical reasons, refer to <u>beating dead horses</u>.

What it means – What you sound like when you repeat the same thing over and over. It probably doesn't have the same impact it once did because only collectors and music snobs own records anymore, but it just doesn't work to say, "like a broken CD" or, even more nonsensical, "like a broken MP3 file."

What it used to mean – "The copy of *Hotel California* I bought at The Wherehouse is scratched! I damn well better get my money back."

Bromance (n.)

Who uses it – Writers at pop culture magazines. The same ones who gave us Brangelina, TomKat, Billary, Bennifer and Kimye.

What it means – A relationship between two guys who get along so well they look like they might be gay, but they're not. Or between two homophobic guys who *are* gay but want to stay in the closet.

What it sounds like – The brand name for a shaving cream or seltzer.

Budding (adj.)

Who uses it – Journalists who subconsciously wish their significant other would buy them flowers. Just once.

What it means – Sometimes referred to as the "next big thing." Something new and exciting that has yet to reach its potential but is sure to do so in the not-too-distant future. "How do we know? Because we're really good at predicting things, that's how. Didn't we tell you soccer would be bigger than the NFL in the United States by 1990? That disco would last forever? That mullets and bell bottoms were transcendent? Well, forget all that, because we're right *this time*. Just trust us."

What it used to mean – Something that happens to a flower before it blooms.

Bull in a china shop (n.)

Who uses it – Anyone except china shop owners, none of whom, it's safe to say, have ever had one of these animals on their premises.

What it means – An individual who is reckless and prone to making a mess of things.

What it sounds like – An animal you don't want to take by the horns or pair with the elephant in the room.

Bullish (adj.)

Who uses it – Investors who don't like the word "optimistic."

What it means – Optimistic; the opposite of "bearish." You won't find bovines in a bull market, which might lead you to ask, "Where's the beef?" Especially when prices are artificially inflated, in which case the bull market really is a load of bull. The only thing a bull market has in common with an actual bull is that they both involve stock (livestock on the one hand, corporate shares on the other).

What it sounds like – Whoever came up with this term was a former cowboy. Something out of an old Merrill Lynch ad.

Burn the candle at both ends (v.)

Who uses it – Motivational speakers who stress the importance of "caring for yourself" even though you've got three jobs and still can't pay the rent. Candlemakers who want you to use their product faster so you can buy more.

What it means – Getting up early and staying up late to accomplish a task, or to party, or both.

What it sounds like – Absurd. When's the last time

you went to a candle store and saw a candle with a wick sticking out of both ends? I'm waiting.

Butthurt (adj.)

Who uses it – Bullies trying to make their targets feel weak. Action heroes. Football coaches.

What it means – Easily offended. Whiny. A condition that allegedly arises in people who refuse to man up and grow a pair.

What it sounds like – "You've been sitting on that bench too long. Get up, or you'll get blood clots in your legs." Or: "A mule just kicked you in the hindquarters," in which case you should probably get to a hospital (and find someone else to drive you; preferably an ambulance so you can lie down).

By the book (adv.)

Who uses it – Authority figures incapable of original thought.

What it means – "Don't think outside the box." Then again, you're supposed to do that, too. Just be sure you know when to do one and when to do the other.

That's not in the book. You've got to read your boss' mind to figure it out. Good luck, and go get 'em!

What it sounds like – Something authors want readers to do: buy the book.

Bye, Felicia (intj.)

Who uses it – People too young to remember "Don't let the door hit you on the way out" or "See ya!"

What it means – "Wanna leave? That's fine with us. Good riddance." First used in a 1995 film called *Friday* that grossed just $27 million at the box office. It's a pretty good bet that more people know the saying than saw the movie.

What it sounds like – A pretty mean thing to say to someone named Felicia.

Cautionary tale (n.)

Who uses it – TV news and sports analysts.

What it means – "Someone just screwed up badly. We're going to plaster her face on the screen and repeat her story a hundred times in the next twenty-four hours to make sure you don't forget what an idiot she is." Cautionary tales are frequently told by know-it-alls and accompanied by phrases such as "let this be a lesson to you" and "don't try this at home."

What it sounds like – Self-righteous B.S.

Censorship! (n.)

Who uses it – Social media trolls who've just said something so offensive that nobody wants to hear it, but who accuse anyone who dares to ignore it of trying to censor them.

What it means – An excuse to behave like a jackass. "You *have to listen to me* or you're violating my First Amendment rights!" Sure, we do.

What it used to mean – The Hays Code in Hollywood; McCarthyism; and especially government-run media in places like China, Russia and North Korea.

What it sounds like – An excuse by an insecure person to foist his or her ideas off onto an unwilling audience.

Change agent (n.)

Who uses it – Businesspeople and cable news announcers, sometimes even when talking to each other on camera.

What it means – Someone who doesn't settle for the status quo. Of course, if the status quo is working, this may not be a good thing.

What it sounds like – A character from *Get Smart!* A Realtor or intelligence operative with a particularly large wardrobe.

Charity stripe (n.)

Who uses it – Basketball announcers who are allergic to saying "free-throw line" or "foul line." Perhaps they should be issued a technical foul for using it, because it certainly is foul.

What it means – Free-throw line. But it's a misnomer. A player doesn't get to shoot free throws because the other team is feeling charitable. It happens because the player is the victim of a foul, or the referee decides he is, which isn't always the same thing.

What it sounds like – A mark on a candy striper's uniform at the hospital.

Charm offensive (n.)

Who uses it – Cable news announcers, usually in describing politicians. (Politicians, however, are seldom known to use it in describing cable news announcers.)

What it means – Bullshit barrage. 'Nuff said.

What it sounds like – A manufacturer has decided to flood the market with charm bracelets.

Chat you up (v.)

Who uses it – Nosey people who want to sound friendly; unscrupulous coworkers looking for a chance to steal your ideas.

What it means – Engage in "consultation."

What it sounds like – Phrases like this refer to some direction – up, down, out, around – but have nothing to do with points on the compass. Others include "sound you out," "dress you down," "look you up," "look you over," "beat you up" and so forth. It seems like they should stand in contrast to something, but it doesn't work that way. Dressing someone up isn't the opposite of dressing the person down. It would be rude to look somebody *under*, and it would be plain silly to chat somebody *down* or sound a person *in*. "Chat you up" sounds just as silly.

Chill (intj., v.)

Who uses it – Friends and significant others who are uncomfortable with the fact that you're upset.

What it means – Mellow out. Calm down. Translation: "Stop ranting and whining about your problems. You're stressing me out. And don't you know *I'm* the important person here? I don't care about your problems anyway. I just pretend to because that's what a friend (or spouse) is supposed to do. So shut the hell up. Now." Variants: Chill out, take a chill pill.

What it used to mean – Something that happens during a sub-freezing night in the orange grove, inside a meat locker or at a Green Bay Packers game in December.

Chilling (adj.)

Who uses it – The same people who use "stunning;" e.g., cable news anchors and reporters, often used as an adjective describing "effect."

What it means – A handy-dandy word to use in describing a government action or court decision that restricts someone from doing something. For example, "this ruling will have a chilling effect on free speech."

What it used to mean – Something done when you

make popsicles or want beer to be ready to consume by game time.

Circle back (v.)

Who uses it – Businesspeople who don't think you've explained yourself well enough or progressed far enough on a project. Folks who like to beat dead horses.

What it means – Revisit a subject later.

What it used to mean – Something a military scout did after scoping out the enemy camp. Even then, it wasn't an actual circle, but more like a half-circle – an indirect route used to avoid detection.

What it sounds like – Something that happens on a teacup ride at an amusement park; it'll make you dizzy just thinking about it. Not in any way associated with the hardcore punk band Circle Jerks.

Coffers (n.)

Who uses it – Print journalists trying to save print space by using three narrow characters – f, f and r – in the span of seven letters (the same people who used to use "solons" in place of "legislators" because it fit better in headlines, then realized the term had become so archaic that readers thought they were referring to Old West taverns.)

What it means – Where corporations and political action committees keep their money, as opposed to the rest of us, who keep it in banks, a cookie jar or stuffed in a mattress. Often referring to a mysterious, indeterminate location, such as an offshore account or Switzerland.

What it sounds like – Involuntary physical reactions by people who smoke a lot or have chest colds.

Collateral damage (n.)

Who uses it – Heartless military commanders and even more heartless politicians.

What it means – People got hurt because you didn't care enough about them to consider how something might affect them. Calling them "collateral damage" is a way of justifying your decision, because it's a hell of a lot easier than apologizing or admitting that maybe you were either shortsighted or a downright ass.

What it used to mean – The same thing, but limited to a military context. Alternately, a 2002 movie starring Arnold Schwarzenegger.

Comfort zone (n.)

Who uses it – Motivational speakers who, for whatever reason, don't like people.

What it means – A place you're told you need to get out of. Even if you're wrapped in a nice cozy quilt, drinking a cup of hot chocolate with a cat curled up in your lap, listening to your favorite tunes. Especially then.

What it sounds like – A place you want to stay. Especially if you're wrapped in a nice cozy quilt, drinking a cup of hot chocolate with a cat curled up in your lap, listening to your favorite tunes.

Cool beans (intj.)

Who uses it – The generation after the one that coined the term "cool," no doubt influenced by the popularity of bean dip (yuck).

What it means – Your roommate brought back leftovers from that Mexican food joint up the road and left them out on the counter for you. Of course, he ate the entrees and left you with only the refried beans and a little Spanish rice. Which are cold and not cool at all.

What it sounds like – A recipe for food poisoning.

Copacetic (adj.)

Who uses it – A street hustler who carries around hot knockoffs of designer watches and other "fine" jewelry inside his overcoat.

What it means – "We're in the clear. The cops are looking the other way."

What it sounds like – Something Al Pacino might say in a mob movie. What Al Capone might have said about the empty vault Geraldo opened on national TV. Or a brand of cough syrup.

Core competency (n.)

Who uses it – Business types who are too self-important to speak in plain English.

What it means – The thing you're best at doing.

What it sounds like – Pretentious. The most important quality of the worm that burrowed into your apple, making itself the core of your problem.

Couch potato (n.)

Who uses it – People who like to pretend they don't like couches or potatoes. (Because really, who doesn't like these things?)

What it means – A slob who sits around all day and accomplishes nothing beyond staring at the TV screen, drinking beer and munching on chips.

What it sounds like – You got messy while eating potato chips on the couch, and some of the pieces fell between the cushions. Once there, they grew stale and eventually attracted fire ants that bit you in the ass, causing you to cry out in pain and leap to your feet, thereby curing you of being a couch potato – at least for a few hours.

Cougar (n.)

Who uses it – Men who secretly want a relationship with an "experienced" woman because they're afraid of becoming 40-year-old virgins. Women who like younger men but don't like to be accused of "robbing the cradle." ("Cougar" somehow sounds a lot less offensive and a lot more dangerous at the same time.)

What it means – A middle-aged or older woman who enjoys pursuing and dating younger men. Why a cougar and not a sloth, armadillo or chipmunk? Would any woman (or a guy, for that matter) really want to be compared to any of those animals?

What it used to be called – Robbing the cradle.

What it used to mean – A mountain lion, puma or catamount: a big cat that ranges across the Americas. Also, a member of one of 27 collegiate athletic programs across the United States, most prominently at Brigham Young, Houston and Washington State universities. (Not to mention two defunct professional teams: the Detroit Cougars of the National Hockey League and the Carolina Cougars of the American Basketball Association).

Cray-cray (adj.)

Who uses it – Why would anyone want to?

What it means – Crazy, for people allergic to the letter "z."

What it sounds like – A young child who wants to color but hasn't figured out how to say "crayon."

Creation science (n.)

Who uses it – Christians who don't accept the

theory of evolution.

What it means – An alternative to evolution, given added credibility (its users hope) by the inclusion of the word "science" which supposedly sounds a lot better than the *theory* of evolution. Please don't call it creationism, which became a negative term about the time people realized it shared a suffix with such terms as racism, sexism, communism, paganism, socialism and – perhaps worst of all – rationalism. Blasphemy!

What it sounds like – A load of hooey.

Crunch time (n.)

Who uses it – Coaches, sports announcers. Personal trainers who think it's time to do some stomach crunches. People who test trash compacters. People who recycle aluminum cans.

What it means – In athletic events: "It's really important that you play well now, because it's all on the line. This ignores the fact that, had the athlete(s) performed better before it got to this point, there wouldn't be a crunch time because the other team would already have been crunched like a handful of cheese puffs in the mouth of a hungry six-year-old.

What it sounds like – A bone breaking.

Cuck (n.)

Who uses it – Men (mostly) who want to impugn a rival's masculinity by suggesting his wife/girlfriend is sleeping around ... and he's oblivious about what's happening.

What it means – "You're a weak, impotent, clueless git." Someone who's allegedly subservient to a manipulative/overbearing partner. It's derived from the name of the cuckoo, which lays its eggs in other birds' nests and leaves the unwitting mother bird to raise them. There's a female version of this, too, called a cuckquean, but it's doubtful you've ever heard of it, because men tend to dish out this particular variety of degrading bullshit a lot more often than women do. Lately, the term has become trendy in politics for bashing someone accused of being too weak to stand up for hard-core principles. Particularly on the extreme right, which dismisses mainstream conservatives as "cuckservatives."

What it sounds like – Crude and highly inappropriate in polite company.

Cultural appropriation (n.)

Who uses it – Activists who believe one culture (usually the dominant culture) shouldn't make use of styles and innovations created by another culture.

What it means – It's hard to say. Dreadlocks are off limits. There's a huge debate over the use of Native American names for sports teams, although "Redskins" seems like a no-brainer. (Should we have teams called the Blackskins, Whiteskins, Yellowskins and Purpleskins? I think not.) But no one seems to have any problem with people eating at a fast-food taco chain, even though it's owned by a big American corporation and what's served there has about as much in common with traditional Mexican food as something served under a couple of yellowish arches.

What it sounds like – De facto plagiarism if you're profiting from it (white singers making a killing off of black artists' compositions in the early to mid-20th century) or claiming it's somehow original. Bigotry if you're lampooning it, ala the Cleveland Indians' longtime mascot or people performing in blackface. As long as you're paying royalties, treating the subject with respect and giving credit where credit is due, you shouldn't be accused of this. But that doesn't mean you won't be.

What it used to mean – I was growing a culture of mold in my lab, and a rival scientist stole it! Curses!

Currently (adv.)

Who uses it – Journalists and writers who don't trust the present tense to do its job and/or think it sounds more impressive than "now" (which is overused, too).

What it means – An adverb referring to the present state of affairs. But when used as part a sentence that's already in the present tense, it's usually redundant: "I am currently at home." Why not just say, "I'm at home"? The only reason to use "currently" (or "now") in a present-tense sentence is to create a contrast that isn't otherwise obvious: "I was at the store, but I'm currently home" or "I'm at home now, but I'll be going to the store in a few minutes."

What it sounds like – Overkill.

Cutting edge (n.)

Who uses it – Marketing departments; only truly applicable if they're selling razorblades, scissors, broadswords, battleaxes or guillotines.

What it means – That imaginary place where the "next big thing" resides. Often applied to technology that "authorities" declare to be better than everything else on the market, even though it has yet to be fully tested or embraced by consumers.

What it sounds like – The land where Betamax resided before it was consigned to the imaginary dustbin of history (aka the scrapheap), soon to be joined by eight-tracks, cassette tapes, typewriters, phone booths (sorry, Superman), dot-matrix printers, rotary-dial phones and pagers. And, yes, by VHS, the format that beat out Betamax to begin with, long since swept aside by DVD, Blu-Ray and streaming video.

Dank (adj.)

Who uses it – Stoners. People who want to sound like stoners because they think stoners sound cool, even though they themselves don't smoke weed.

What it means – Good. In the same way that "bad" supposedly meant "good" around the time Michael Jackson released an album of that title. (Yeah, I already used that example, but it's just so damned appropriate.)

What it used to mean – Damp and musty; stale.

Not good at all.

What it sounds like – Dracula's wine cellar.

Data-driven (adj.)

Who uses it – Businesspeople who want to make it seem like their ideas are based on something more than their own guesswork and adolescent fantasies.

What it means – "Of course, this is better than mere conjecture and pseudo-science. You believe me ... don't you?"

What it sounds like – The Enterprise D when helmed by Lt. Cmdr. Data.

Debbie downer (n.)

Who uses it – Comedians, way too often.

What it means – Someone who's no fun to be around. This phrase is not only annoying, it perpetuates a false stereotype that such people are usually women. I know otherwise, since I can be one, and I'm decidedly male.

What it sounds like – Someone bought a package

of Little Debbie cookies past the expiration date and is suffering by having to sit *down.* A lot. In the lavatory.

Decimate (v.)

Who uses it – Reporters who mastered fractions but were stumped by decimals.

What it means – "A lot of shit was destroyed. Maybe almost all of it."

What it used to mean – Destroying ten percent of something.

What it sounds like – Reporters aren't good at math (most of them will admit as much). But critics might say they are good at decimating the language: misusing, overusing or rendering meaningless roughly ten percent of what they write.

Deep state (n.)

Who uses it – Conspiracy theorists. The kind of people who believe the Earth is flat, Barack Obama was born in Kenya and no one ever landed on the moon. (Didn't you know that climate change is a fraud dreamed up by members of the Illuminati and Marilyn Manson fans who want to brainwash us using chemtrails, toxic vaccines, "backwards masking" and an endless barrage of old Rick Astley videos?)

What it means – A fictional cabal that exists in the minds of paranoid partisans who are convinced that people are plotting to undermine them from within. Within what? Their own imaginations. Related to the "vast right-wing conspiracy" against the Clintons. The truth is out there. But you won't find it by listening to these folks.

What it sounds like – An intense level of meditation. One so profound and all-encompassing that you forget how to think altogether.

Deosil (n.)

Who uses it – Pagans, Wiccans and other Earth religions.

What it means – Clockwise. It means clockwise. They just use a different word for it to make it sound ancient and mysterious.

What it sounds like – An anti-perspirant.

Detail-oriented (adj.)

Who uses it – People who aren't what this describes, or they'd have taken note of the detail that this phrase is so overused that it has become virtually meaningless.

What it means – Obsessively anal. Someone who will be a micromanager if put in a position with even the slightest authority.

What it sounds like – An accountant. Someone who generates fine print for legal documents. Ebenezer Scrooge before his enlightenment.

Dive deep (v.)

Who uses it – Cable news talking heads who are paid to make shallow analysis sound like it's the most profound insight since the theory of relativity.

What it means – See "drill down" and "unpack" further on (I'm trying to make sure you read the whole book).

What it used to mean – Something to do with Jacques Cousteau. If you don't remember who he was, look it up. Or listen to the John Denver tune *Calypso.* Or both.

Digital footprint (n.)

Who uses it – Self-proclaimed experts in SEO (search engine optimization) who want to sound as if they know how to increase your website's visibility, when it really all depends on Google's and Facebook's whim of the moment ... and these "experts" just want to take your money.

What it means – A marker that enables someone to trace where you've been and what you've said or done online. Big Brother is watching you.

What it used to mean – It wasn't used prior to the computer age, but if it had been, it would have referred to the impression made by one's toes, most ideally – though not necessarily – in the white sand on a glorious sunny day at the beach (the toes being the digits on one's feet).

Dizzying array (n.)

Who uses it – Announcers and writers who aren't dizzy, even though they contend to have seen such an array.

What it means – An incredible variety.

What it sounds like – Such a vast assortment of things that you can't take it all in without suffering from a severe sense of vertigo, kind of like what happens when you're falling-down drunk. (But really, when's the last time you *remember* that happening?)

Don the mantle (v.)

Who uses it – Fantasy writers and political analysts, who aren't necessarily the same people (but sometimes are).

What it means – Taking a leadership role previously filled by someone else.

What it sounds like – Some bizarre combination of Don Quixote and Mickey Mantle.

Don't drink the Kool-Aid (intj.)

Who uses it – People who want you to think you're being brainwashed by a cult, either because they're genuinely concerned about your well-being or because they want to brainwash you themselves.

What it means – Someone's trying to persuade you not to do something that will hurt you.

What it sounds like – Kool-Aid might be harmful to diabetics because of all that sugar, and it might not be as good for kids as milk, but that's not what this means.

What it originally meant – In late 1978, cult leader Jim Jones poisoned a batch of fruit punch and gave it to his followers at their failed paradise in Guyana, South America, killing more than 900 people. It was the largest loss of civilian American life in a single event until the September 11 terrorist attacks of 2001. It wasn't even Kool-Aid, but a different brand. Leave it to pop culture to turn a tragedy into a catchphrase – and get the details wrong in the process.

Dog (n.)

Who uses it – Canine lovers in describing their friends, even though those friends aren't canines. Sometimes spelled as "dawg," for no apparent reason.

What it means – "I like my dog, and a dog is man's best friend. You're my best friend, so even though you're not a dog, I'll call you one." Similar to homie, homeboy. An aging bounty hunter who was the focus of a cable TV reality show for eight seasons.

What it sounds like – A lot better than calling a woman a bitch, which used to mean a female dog but is acceptable if a woman uses it as a term of self-empowerment.

What it used to mean – Scooby-Doo, Snoopy, Goofy, Pluto. A golden retriever. A poodle. A Chihuahua.

A Saint Bernard. An animal that eats kibble and isn't a cat. You get the picture.

Dope (adj.)

Who uses it – People too cool to say "cool."

What it means – Cool (but not as it relates to temperature). Awesome. Really out of the ordinary in a special, positive kind of way

What it used to mean – Marijuana. Before that, a stupid person, which doesn't seem to make much sense in light of its more recent meaning, unless you think Homer Simpson, Beavis, Joey from *Friends* and Jar Jar Binks are simultaneously extremely smart and extremely cool.

Double down (v.)

Who uses it – Journalists who have spent too much time in Vegas. Why do they love this term so much? Because it's another way of making something sound more important, dangerous, daring or rebellious than it really is. Translation: higher ratings, please!

What it means – To keep saying something stupid after it's been exposed as stupid on the assumption that, if you repeat it often enough, it will sound less stupid. What really happens: You sound more stupid – about as stupid as the political commentators who use this phrase so often they expose their own limited vocabulary and lack of verbal creativity.

What it used to mean – A strategy in blackjack and other casino games in which you double your bet because you're confident you have a winning hand. To be fair, there is some correlation here: This is often stupid, too.

Douchebag (n.)

Who uses it – Someone seeking to impugn the reputation of another by comparing him (it's usually a "him") to a feminine hygiene product.

What it means – A self-important jackass.

What it used to mean – A bag holding fluid used during a douche (the process of rising a body cavity, most often the vagina). This should not to be confused with a deuce, which is a playing card or another name for the number two ... although the two words are frequently confused while listening to Manfred Mann's hit *Blinded by the Light.* Douche rhymes with cartouche, a carved tablet adorned with hieroglyphs that tends to be a lot more durable than a douche.

Downsize (v.)

Who uses it – Corporations that want to appease shareholders and, at the same time, fool employees into thinking they're doing something positive. It's effective in doing the first, but not the second.

What it means – "Our stockholders aren't making enough money to justify their overinvestment in our firm, so we'll have to cut staff and other resources so we can produce less and make them even more unhappy with the results. But at least they won't be spending as much."

What it used to mean – Moving from a suburban ranch house into a smaller home after the kids flew the coop. What happened to the unfortunate protagonist of *The Incredible Shrinking Man* or to Rick Moranis' offspring in *Honey, I Shrunk the Kids.*

Dramatic (adj.)

Who uses it – Cable news announcers like Wolf Blitzer, often followed by the words "new development." You might call such announcers drama kings and queens, except there are so many of them it's more proper to call them drama serfs and vassals.

What it means – Something similar to "breaking

news," used every now and then as an alternative to keep viewers on their toes and give them the impression that something even more groundbreaking or revolutionary is about to be reported.

What it used to mean – A stage performance of something like a Shakespearean play. No offense to Wolf Blitzer, but he's no Shakespeare.

Drill down (v.)

Who uses it – The same talking heads who use dive deep, for the same reason.

What it means – To go deeper and probe the true essence of a subject. Most commonly used by cable news analysts who really don't know much more about the subject than they've already said, but who need to fill time in their 24-hour news cycle by asking the same questions repeatedly to a rotating panel of the same talking heads, who pop up on the screen to contradict one another so frequently that you feel like you're watching a game of whack-a-mole.

What it used to mean – Something a dentist does to your teeth, which is only moderately more pleasant than watching cable news 24 hours a day.

What it used to mean, too – Something people do

when they're looking for oil. This usage has fallen out of favor, no doubt, because alternative forms of energy have gained traction. People still drill for oil, but they don't talk about it, the same way people don't talk about listening to '90s boy bands or ordering anchovies on their pizza.

Ducks in a row (n.)

Who uses it – An individual trying to scare you into thinking you haven't done enough to prepare for what that person considers an Armageddon-level reckoning: "You'd better get your ducks in a row!"

What it means – Prepared. Ready to go. Something you want to be.

What it used to mean – At a shooting gallery, two-dimensional ducks parade across a bucolic yet cartoonish background, daring you to shoot them with your trusty air rifle. These aren't just ducks in a row, they're sitting ducks. Not something you want to be.

Dude! (intj.)

Who uses it – People, often from Southern California, some of whom are referred to as "surfer dudes."

What it means – An expression of surprise, dismay or some combination of the two. The exclamation point is mandatory, and it's common (but optional) to draw it out as "Duuuude!" It doesn't matter whether the person being addressed is literally a dude (guy) or has ever worked on a dude ranch – which has nothing to do with surfing unless you've got an amazingly talented, water-loving horse.

What it sounds like – You're a fan of *Fast Times at Ridgemont High*, the Bill and Ted movies or *Wayne's World*. Or you want to emulate Jeff Bridges' character in *The Big Lebowski* – in which case, you abide.

Due diligence (n.)

Who uses it – Lawyers or businesspeople who want you to think they take everything super-seriously, so they behave superciliously. The same people who use "best practices" and make a big deal about going by the book.

What it means – You've done everything possible to avoid giving anyone an excuse to sue you. (If you forget this, just remember that "sue" rhymes with "due.")

What it sounds like – Being sure to return that novel to the library by its due date, because you're afraid of ringing up hundreds of dollars in late fees for a book that has coffee stains on the pages and a cracked spine that makes it worth no more than a nickel.

Dustbin of history (n.)

Who uses it – Political analysts eager to write off ideas they don't like as obsolete. Fired janitors.

What it means – Where obsolete ideas go to die.

What it sounds like – Anything not happening now is irrelevant, right? History is a dustbin, and anything from the past that doesn't affect us directly in the present is, therefore ... dust. That is to say, unworthy of our attention. People who use this phrase may not realize that it was coined by the Russian revolutionary Leon Trotsky, who was later assassinated on the order of Joseph Stalin but who, despite this, did not pass into the dustbin of history. History is eco-friendly: It doesn't have a dustbin, but a recycle bin. Better quotes include "There is nothing new under the sun" from the Book of Ecclesiastes and "Those who cannot remember the past are condemned to repeat it" by George Santayana.

Early-morning hours (n.)

Who uses it – Reporters. It's their favorite time of day. How do we know? Because they use it so damned often (especially in crime stories).

What it means – Early in the morning, a time during which (as with any other time), there are hours. There are also minutes and seconds, but reporters never refer to "early-morning minutes." Nor do they refer to "late-night hours." It's just "late at night" or, more commonly, an actual time. Gasp! Specificity! What a concept! Occasionally, a reporter will deviate from this template and refer to the "pre-dawn hours," which is just as bad. It doesn't add drama to the story. It doesn't make the reporter's narrative sound as though it came from the mouth of Rod Serling introducing an episode of *The Twilight Zone* or the pages of a Mickey Spillane detective novel. It just sounds ...

What it sounds like – Stupid. It just sounds stupid.

Earworm (n.)

Who uses it – Anyone referring to "It's a Small World," "YMCA," "The Lollipop Guild," "500 Miles," "The Girl from Ipanema," "Tubthumping" and other songs that are so infectious they've become plagues upon humanity.

What it means – A song you can't get out of your head.

What it sounds like – A worm that deposits itself in one's ear. Disgusting, eh? It's been used repeatedly on social media by actor George Takei, who once appeared in a movie (*Star Trek II: The Wrath of Khan*) where a worm *was* deposited into another character's ear. The term originally referred to bugs called earwigs that live in dark areas like fallen logs and crevices; according to an old folk belief, they were prone to crawling into a person's ear canal. That belief that was later debunked but may have been the inspiration for the use of the term in this small world of ours.

Elephant in the room (n.)

Who uses it – Cable news anchors. Fans of Dumbo and Babar who don't think they get the recognition they deserve.

What it means – Something very big and very important that everyone chooses to ignore because it's awkward or controversial.

What it used to mean – Hannibal (the Carthaginian general, not the fictional cannibal) and his army are spending the night at your house.

What it sounds like – Time to put away the breakables, especially if the room happens to be in a china shop and a bull is added to the mix.

Embattled (adj.)

Who uses it – Journalists who like to make ordinary conflicts seem more historically significant by using the language of warfare. Writers who never learned the principle of "show, don't tell."

What it means – Engaged in a battle or controversy. If you're an elected official whose actions are being heavily criticized, who's involved in some scandal or who's the target of even a potential investigation, chances are you're "embattled." At least according to the journalism industry, which has more than 170,000 English words at its disposal but likes to use this particular adjective more than most of the rest put together. Most politicians really are *embattled* at some point, so is that vague detail even newsworthy? Give us the juicy details and stop repeating what we already know.

What it used to mean – A situation that occurs when fighting with swords and spears or bayonets or cannons. That's a lot more interesting than politicians insulting one another ... at least most of the time.

Entitled (adj.)

Who uses it – Baby boomers who think the current generation feels entitled to a life of video games, free room and board, partying late and sleeping in. Basically: "spoiled" applied to a broader audience than brats and only-children (of which I'm one).

What it means – "These kids today! In my day, I walked ten miles to school in a blizzard, then had to walk home with blisters on my feet and do three hours of hard labor. If I didn't, I got taken out to the woodshed, and Pops used a 2-by-4 with a rusty nail at the end of it to whup my backside."

What it sounds like – Perhaps a little green monster is rearing its ugly head?

Explosive (adj.)

Who uses it – Cable news types trying to indicate how important, groundbreaking or controversial a development is.

What it means – At least the speaker has the decency to use a word that was meant to be used primarily as an adjective. Unlike "bombshell."

What it used to mean – Detonation followed by a big kaboom!

Exponential (adj.)

Who uses it – Reporters who aren't mathematicians, the same ones who love "decimate."

What it means – "Oh, wow! Something increased by a whole lot. We don't know by how much, and we know the average person doesn't know the true definition of 'exponential,' but neither do we. So, no harm done, right? Any mathematicians out there have more important things to do than watch our banal newscast and hold us to account for misusing this word."

What it used to mean – Involving an exponent in a mathematical equation (as opposed to a base), commonly expressed as "x to the power of y."

Facepalm (n.)

Who uses it – Lovers of social media who aren't lazy enough to resort to the three-letter alternative, SMH.

What it means – The act of slapping one's self on the forehead with the palm of a hand (hopefully, not too hard) in an expression of extreme frustration at the idiocy in the world around you.

What it sounds like – A palm tree growing out of someone's face.

Facilitate (v.)

Who uses it – People from human resources and the robotic hired guns they bring in to run tedious policy workshops on subjects nobody cares about. Nevertheless, corporations insist they "must" be covered, if only to give you less time for the real work they require of you.

What it means – Make things simpler. Usually, it does the exact opposite.

What it sounds like – When you visit the facilities, you go to the restroom, so it's no wonder that facilitators are so often full of shit.

Failure is not an option (decl.)

Who uses it – Military commanders, coaches and people who want to blame you in advance for something that hasn't happened.

What it means – "Everything depends on you. If you screw this up, I want nothing to do with you. Or it's the end of the world. Or both." It amounts to a guilt trip before the fact. Perhaps even worse, it indicates that whoever's saying this has neglected to come up with a backup plan, in which case 1) failure *would* be an option, 2) you might actually be able to learn from it and 3) the person making the plans would have to take responsibility for them rather than foisting them off on the people left to execute them.

What it sounds like – Something a bully would say, and an unimaginative bully, at that.

Fake news (n.)

Who uses it – The 45th president, his supporters, journalists. People who never learned the term "propaganda."

What it means – Propaganda, but I guess people just don't have the patience for four-syllable words anymore. Just as often: Anything I don't like and want to discredit without going to the trouble of investigating whether it's true or not.

What it used to mean – Nothing, really. No one used to employ this term, and we were infinitely better off. Can we go back to that time? Please?

Fellowship (n.)

Who uses it – Churchgoers.

What it means – The religious equivalent to partying, but without the booze and the flirting. Well, at least without the booze and without flirting that leads to carnal activities. Well, most of the time. Unless someone backslides. Also, something that hobbits and other imaginary folks did with regards to a certain magical ring in J.R.R. Tolkien's stories. The ring, if one is to be believed, was even more tempting than booze and carnal activities. I repeat, *if* one is to be believed. Sometimes, annoyingly, used as a faux verb ("to fellowship").

What it sounds like – A male boat.

Field general (n.)

Who uses it – Sports announcers who don't like the word "quarterback," possibly because they also don't like the band Nickelback, which has nothing to do with football ... unless you count the fifth defensive back inserted to counter two-minute offenses. Usually ineffectively. Nickelback got its name because one of the band members used to work at Starbucks and would give customers a "nickel back" in change. Quarterbacks, on the other hand, have nothing to do with coinage, apart from the fact that they get paid millions of dollars if they play in the National Football League – even though they have no experience in the military as actual field generals.

What it means – A quarterback. Particularly an effective one who knows how to rally the troops and lead them to victory.

What used to mean – A real general on a real battlefield in a real war.

What it sounds like – A bad analogy.

First blush (n.)

Who uses it – Journalists (again) and others who think "first glance" is too much of a cliché but don't want to think hard enough to avoid this only slightly less-worn cliché.

What it means – A first impression.

What it sounds like – What happens the first time you say something embarrassing, or when you have your first taste of a rosé wine.

Feat. or ft. (v.)

Who uses it – Recording artists, often, but not exclusively, on pop and hip-hop releases.

What it means – "I want to name-drop all my famous friends to help me sell this mediocre musical release."

What it sounds like – The record label is too lazy to write out the word "featuring," or doesn't know how to spell it. Or the egotistical artist wants to save space to make his name bigger. Or someone thinks it looks cool. Probably all three.

Feeding frenzy (n.)

Who uses it – Most often, people describing how reporters or fans descend on celebrities.

What it means – Those doing the feeding are hungry for comments (if they're reporters), pictures (if they're paparazzi), autographs (if they're fans) or just a glimpse of someone famous. No food is actually served or eaten, unless this occurs at a restaurant, in which case the consumption of food is incidental to what the phrase describes.

What it sounds like – A scene from Jaws. Or what happens when a dead animal falls into a school of piranha.

Feminazis (n.)

Who uses it – Rush Limbaugh's dittoheads and other assorted misogynists.

What it means – People who want equal rights for women are just on the same level as supporters of Hitler. Which is kind of like saying Lassie is on the same level as a rabid wolf. Or Julia Child is the equivalent of Hannibal Lecter.

What it sounds like – The kind of propaganda that Joseph Goebbels might have shunned as over the top, but hey, it works in Merica.

Fever pitch (n.)

Who uses it – Writers and journalists trying to inject drama into their narrative. Then again, that might just be fevered speculation.

What it means – A crescendo. The place that something rises to just before it reaches a tipping point.

What it sounds like – A pitcher takes the mound with a high body temperature. A baritone tries to sing in the same condition and ends up sounding like a soprano not named Tony.

Fixer (n.)

Who uses it – Journalists, but only since the 45th president took office. Crime novelists. FBI agents. Mob bosses.

What it means – A person who cleans up all your messes. Not a janitor or a nanny paid to change your diapers, but if you need to keep someone on staff to do this full time, you really ought to think about changing from cloth to Huggies or Pampers.

What used to mean – A chemical mix used in processing photographs, but few people remember this since everything's gone digital.

What it sounds like – A handyman (but not the kind mentioned in the James Taylor song of that title).

Flesh it out (v.)

Who uses it – Someone who wants to circle back to a subject later.

What it means – "Anyone could have come up with that simplistic idea! Come back when you've got something substantial to show me."

What it sounds like – A mad scientist has a skeleton in his closet. He removes some organs from jars of formaldehyde that have been lining the back wall and inserts them into the body cavities. He starts grafting muscle and sinew and tendon onto the bones. He sprays silly string on it and wraps it in duct tape. ... but all he ends up with is a disgusting mess. (Not to be confused with "flush it out," which is something you do when you have a foreign object in your eye, like a cinder block or an eighteen-wheeler).

Flip (v.)

Who uses it – People who speak "modern-day presidential."

What it means – A person who's in trouble with the law and is offered a plea deal or immunity in exchange for information/testimony against a bigger fish the government wants to fry.

What used to mean – Something Nadia Comaneci, Simone Biles and Mary Lou Retton did in the Olympics. A comedian in the 1970s named Wilson, known for playing a character named Geraldine.

What it sounds like – You're craving pancakes.

For all intents and purposes

(adv.)

Who uses it – Overly verbose people, especially political analysts.

What it means – "Practically speaking." This sounds like a hedge – not the kind you find in your yard; the kind you use to avoid speaking with certainty about something in case you're wrong, because you don't want to look like a dolt. It sounds like a hedge, but it's not. It's a definitive statement. You're not talking about *some* intents and purposes, but all of them. You're even being redundant in your certainty, because, the last time I looked, intents were the same thing as purposes. Is this what you're really intending to say? Are you saying it on purpose? Unless you mean to say you know something beyond a shadow of a doubt, you'd best think twice about prefacing an assertion with this phrase.

What it sounds like – For all intensive purposes ... which might make more sense, because it would eliminate the redundancy and make the statement more, well, intense. Be that as it may, that isn't how the saying goes.

Fraught with meaning (adj.)

Who uses it – Pompous, self-important types who probably don't know the definition of "fraught" and have never used the word in any other context.

What it means – "Fraught" means "filled." Why not just say "filled" with meaning? Because it doesn't sound as impressive. Still, no one would ever say his mug is fraught with beer, although it would then be fraught with draught. The two words don't rhyme, despite their similar spelling, so even *that* doesn't work as a source of amusement. The phrase is, therefore, entirely pointless.

What it sounds like – Brought. Sought. Cal Worthington's dog Spot. (This last reference will leave those who grew up outside Southern California scratching their heads, but I don't care.)

Friendzone (n.)

Who uses it – Embittered men who can't handle being rejected and think friendship with anyone of the opposite sex is pointless if you don't wind up in bed.

What it means – That place to which a person with romantic intentions is banished by someone who does not share those intentions.

What it used to be called – Unrequited love.

What it sounds like – A happy place where football players go if they don't want to be competitive. Right.

Freudian slip (n.)

Who uses it – Anyone except someone actually trained in Freudian psychoanalysis.

What it means – A slip of the tongue that reveals one's true thoughts or intentions despite the person's determination to keep them secret.

What it sounds like – An undergarment worn by

Martha Bernays, the wife of Sigmund Freud.

Game face (n.)

Who uses it – Coaches, motivational speakers and business executives.

What it means – "I know we haven't trained you properly, so you don't have a clue what you're talking about. But the company's counting on you to make the sale, so you've got to put on your game face so you look like you're an expert. Or you're fired. Got it?"

What it used to mean – The same thing, except for athletes.

-gate (suff.)

Who uses it – Journalists too young to remember Watergate but too unoriginal to come up with another way of saying "political scandal."

What it means – A name for any and every scandal and political crisis since Watergate, which had nothing to do with water or a gate (it's the name of an office building that's part of a similarly named complex in Washington, D.C.).

What it sounds like ... could be pretty silly given the proper circumstances. A scandal involving the University of Florida might be Gatorgate. The Norse goddess Frigg might be the focus of Frigate. Bill Gates could become embroiled in Gatesgate. Coalminers? Try Coalgate (without fluoride). A cleric who wears stockings? That would be Legate. A Navy admiral? Navigate. A farmer with keen hearing? Irrigate. A stockbroker under scrutiny by the SEC? Investigate. A woman who tries to break her lover out of prison during a conjugal visit? You guessed it: Conjugate.

General consensus (n.)

Who uses it – Analysts trying to sound more important than they are while using extra syllables to fill airtime.

What it means – That you don't know the meaning of the term "consensus," which means "general agreement" (unless you're referring to a high-ranking military officer named Consensus, in which case you should have capitalized the C).

What it used to mean – The same thing it means now: that you should consider taking a course in remedial English.

Gestalt (n.)

Who uses it – Political analysts who flunked out before they could complete their degree in sociology, but who want to sound like they did anyway.

What it means – The general quality or character of something. Want to project an air of expertise by using a foreign word that sounds more complicated than it is? This one fits the bill perfectly. Maybe you get it confused with "zeitgeist." Maybe you mistakenly remember hearing it on an old episode of *Hogan's Heroes*. Regardless, it's one of those slippery words you might have to look up in the dictionary every time you hear it because its definition is so bland that you can't believe anyone would use such a highfalutin word in reference to something so mundane.

What it sounds like – A term Sigmund Freud might use in describing an Oedipal complex, or a table seasoning (pass gestalt and der pepper).

Get 'er done (intj.)

Who uses it – Coaches, military commanders, executives and others who rely on subordinates to do the real work while they watch from the sidelines and reap the benefits.

What it means – "I don't have any instructions for you, because I don't know what the hell I'm doing. I may have hired you because I thought you were dumber than I am, but you've got to be smarter now. If you're not, I'll replace you with someone who *does* know enough to figure this shit out ... but will keep it a secret so I get all the credit."

What it sounds like – Something a Neanderthal might have said.

Get with the program (intj.)

Who uses it – Controlling assholes in all walks of life.

What it means – Someone in a position of authority has decided *this* is how it's going to be. Don't question it. Even if you have a better idea, it will never happen because you're definitely *not* in a position of authority.

What it sounds like – Abuse of power. Tyranny.

Glass half full (n., adj.)

Who uses it – Motivational speakers, preachers.

What it means – Optimistic. Bullish. Not half-empty, even though that's the same thing.

What it sounds like – It won't be long before you'll have to ask the bartender for another round.

Gnarly (adj.)

Who uses it – California kids who want to sound like they're refugees from *Fast Times at Ridgemont High*, *National Lampoon's Vacation* or half a dozen John Hughes films from the 1980s. Like, Omigod! Fer sure! Gag me with a spoon! Totally grody to the max!

What it means – Tubular, righteous, awesome, rad, etc.

What it used to mean – A description of that twisted old tree that grew near the house that was supposed to be haunted. No doubt by fans of *Fast Times at Ridgemont High*, John Hughes movies and Moon Zappa.

GOAT (acr., n.)

Who uses it – Sports journalists who must think it's too much trouble to say "all-time greatest" or "best ever."

What it means – An acronym for "Greatest Of All Time," used primarily by sports journalists.

What it used to mean – The worst, also used primarily by sports journalists. No kidding. Until recently, this term was applied to athletes who messed up so badly and so conspicuously that they either became laughing stocks or caused their teams to lose a championship: players who shot into their own net, ran toward their own goal line or dropped an easy fly ball that would have been the last out in the World Series. All that changed a few years ago, though. Now, the GOAT is a good guy. Next thing you know, they'll create an acronym for WIN that means "Worst In the Nation."

What it used to mean, too – A cloven-hoofed farm animal with spooky eyes that eats tin cans. Often viewed with suspicion, this unfortunate relative of the cute and wooly lamb has been maligned as the repository for all of humanity's ills (a scapegoat). It's even depicted as a symbol of Lucifer, who, come to think of it, is said to have fancied himself the greatest of all time. Coincidence? I wonder ...

Go Dutch (v.)

Who uses it – Cheapskates.

What it means – "I ain't payin' for your food, sucker."

But what if ... You're ordering Belgian waffles, English muffins, Scotch whiskey, French fries, Champagne, hamburgers or Italian sausage? Does that mean you have to treat, since none of these menu items is Dutch?

What it sounds like – A trip to the Netherlands. A rallying cry for Dutch Warmerdam, who held the world record in the pole vault for 17 years in the mid-20th century.

Go-to guy (n.)

Who uses it – Sports analysts and businessmen who seem to believe the most important person on any team is a guy. Tell that to former Olympic standouts like Shannon Miller, Jenny Thompson, Bonnie Blair and Jackie Joyner-Kersee, the dominant forces on various U.S. Olympic teams over the years.

What it means – Someone who can be counted on to complete an assigned task.

What it sounds like – The opposite of a take-from

guy (whatever that is), not to be confused with a goatee guy, who wears a particular style of facial hair, or a GOAT (see above).

Go viral (v.)

Who uses it – Online wannabes longing for their 15 seconds of cyber fame.

What it means – Spread all over the internet. This is viewed as positive, even though a computer virus, which also spreads via the internet, is not positive at all. Part of the distinction involves whether you're the cause of the virus or one of the people it's spread to. Many of the terms mentioned on these pages went viral, and now we're sick of them. Naturally.

What it used to mean – What happens when an infection spreads rapidly, causing widespread death and misery, also known as a plague. This is not viewed as positive in any context, unless you're a psychotic mass murderer or a supervillain in the tradition of Lex Luthor, The Joker, Magneto and Doctor Octopus.

Go yard (v.)

Who uses it – Baseball announcers desperate for yet

another "home run" synonym. As if "four-bagger," "dinger," "round-tripper," "blast" and "touch 'em all!" weren't enough.

What it means – A home run.

What it sounds like – Shorthand for mowing the lawn, recess in elementary school or a trip to the exercise yard at San Quentin.

Grammar Nazi (n.)

Who uses it – People, especially online, who enjoy pointing out other people's English faux pas (even though "faux pas" isn't English) but who cringe whenever someone else corrects *their* mistakes.

What it means – A steadfast guardian of correct grammar, proper spelling and appropriate usage. Or: A know-it-all who feels the need to justify her existence by demonstrating her superiority in the only way she knows how. Often a frustrated author, laid-off newspaper worker or former teacher with too much time on his hands (I may or may not fall into all three of these categories; I'm not saying.) Not to be confused with the Soup Nazi from *Seinfeld*.

What it used to be called – A copy editor, before they became virtually extinct.

What it sounds like – My ninth-grade English teacher.

Graphic novel (n.)

Who uses it – Geeks, nerds and related species.

What it means – This is a pretentious way of talking about what used to be referred to as a "comic book," a term that was, admittedly, inaccurate when referring to a form of literature that routinely deals with such weighty issues as apocalyptic threats and whether one's spandex costume should be red-and-blue or a more menacing black. There isn't too much that's funny about them, except for the Schwarzenegger-like one-liners often placed on the lips of their heroes ... and, of course, those spandex costumes. Some graphic novels are longer than the comic books we bought for a dime or a quarter back in the day, but they're still built around the same characters, most of whom don't age but routinely die, only to reappear in slightly different form in another fictional "universe."

What it sounds like – Someone realized that major movie studios were making billions of dollars from film adaptations of this literature. They couldn't call them "comic books" anymore without exposing them for what they always were: brightly colored mini magazines for kids too old for *Highlights* and too young for *Newsweek*. These days, more adults probably read graphic novels than *Newsweek*, so maybe they're worthy of a more grown-up name after all.

Grimoire (n.)

Who uses it – Pagans, Wiccans and adherents of other Earth religions, particularly those with an affinity for spellcasting.

What it means – A book of spells.

What it sounds like – A collection of fairytales by the Brothers Grimm that's kept in an armoire.

Ground zero (n.)

Who uses it – Television news reporters and, to a slightly lesser extent, print journalists.

What it means – In broad terms, a base for a certain kind of activity. More specifically, a nuclear blast or other cataclysmic event. After the 2001 terrorist attack on New York City, it was used with a capital "Z" so often in reference to the World Trade Center site that it became virtually synonymous with that location.

What it sounds like – An overly dramatic way to

refer to a site where thousands of people lost their lives.

Grow a pair (intj.)

Who uses it – Bullies, coaches, military commanders. Is that redundant?

What it means – Injunction to stand one's ground in an intimidating situation.

What it used to mean – A farmer's wife once needed two more apples to make a pie for Thanksgiving, so she told her husband to do this.

What it sounds like – Sexist as hell.

What it also sounds like – Trying to intimidate someone into not being intimidated. Yeah, like that's gonna work.

Gut check (n.)

Who uses it – Sports announcers and fans, some of whom should perform one of these on their beer bellies.

What it means – Prepare for the worst. Be tough. This is important. And difficult.

What it sounds like – "Someone please measure

my waist. I think I've put on a few pounds." Or "I'm about to barf." Or "I need a doctor's appointment *because* I'm about to barf."

Hack (n.)

Who uses it – Motivational writers and speakers seeking to tell/sell you something you could have figured out on your own.

What it means – A shortcut that's supposed to save you the time and energy you'd otherwise expend in doing it right. Often used as part of the absurd phrase "life hack." A shortcut through life? Really? Personally, I'd rather take my time getting to the end of it. Whatever happened to "stop and smell the roses?" That sounds a lot more pleasant than hacking your way to an early grave.

What it used to mean – A cough so violent as to raise concerns about one's health, often associated with smokers. Fewer people are smoking these days, which means fewer people are hacking. But more people must like the idea of hacking, because they've given it a whole new definition. I don't think Hack Wilson would approve. You've probably heard of Mr. Wilson, which is a shame, because he once hit 56 home runs in a season and set a record for the most runs batted in with 191. The record still stands, but poor Hack is all but forgotten these days, probably because he did it in 1930 ... or maybe because he did it for the Chicago Cubs.

Hallelujah! (intj.)

Who uses it – Church members, and congregations in unison.

What it means – "Praise the Lord!" (which is often used instead by people who prefer English to Hebrew). In practical terms, it's usually just a strong affirmation, the same way "Amen!" is when it's not preceded by a prayer. Also used in the same way: "Preach it!" or simply, "Preach!" Note the exclamation point. It's mandatory, just the way it is in "Dude!" (which is not an acceptable synonym for the Almighty).

What it sounds like – Something a flight attendant might say upon arriving in Hawai'i, along with "Aloha!" and "Mahalo!"

Hashtag (n.)

Who uses it – Twitter users in describing the symbol they employ to spread tweets that no one ever sees anyway (unless they're celebrities with that little blue check by their name).

What it means – "Hey, Mr. Algorithm! Look at me over here! Can I hop on your bandwagon and go viral? Pretty please?"

What it used to be called – A number sign or tic-tac-toe.

What it sounds like – A price tag on your hash browns.

Hat trick (n.)

Who uses it – Hockey announcers. Soccer announcers, too, but only rarely because there's almost never enough scoring in soccer to justify using it.

What it means – The achievement of scoring three goals in a single game.

What it sounds like – A magician's trick, as illustrated when Bullwinkle Moose tried (unsuccessfully) to pull a rabbit out of the hat on the 1960s cartoon *The*

Bullwinkle Show. Thank you, by the way, for indulging all my dated, Baby Boomer pop-culture references.

Haters (n.)

Who uses it – Friends who assure you that these individuals are "gonna hate," as though this is supposed to be reassuring. Still, you end up telling yourself the same thing because you can't think of any other way to feel better when someone is continually harassing, criticizing or attacking you.

What it means – Nasty SOBs. "Haters gonna hate" sounds like the modern equivalent of "nanny nanny nanny goat." Or "sticks and stones may break my bones, but words will never hurt me." Or "I am rubber, you are glue; everything you say bounces off of me and sticks to you."

What it sounds like – About as meaningful as "<u>it is what it is</u>."

Have a heart for (v.)

Who uses it – Evangelical Christians.

What it means – To feel an affinity for a particular cause or ministry. Self-righteous equivalent of "because I felt like it." Other terms such as "called" and "led" may be preferable, because they indicate more clearly it was God's idea and not your own.

What it sounds like – You don't need a coronary transplant.

Headdesk (n.)

Who uses it – Users of online social media who noticed that "facepalm" was losing its impact, so they got more dramatic to keep people paying attention.

What it means – An expression of extreme agitation at something particularly stupid or irrational. Facepalm taken to the next level by smashing your forehead into the desk in front of you. If this in itself seems stupid and irrational, you've grasped the essence of why this word is, well, stupid and irrational.

What it sounds like – Bone hitting wood. It hurts.

Hella (adj.)

Who uses it – California surfers, skateboarders and wannabes.

What it means – Very. Intensely. Extremely.

Probably a condensed version of "that's one hell of a (fill in the blank)," but now often used as a simple adjective in phrases such as "hella good" – which wouldn't make sense as "hell of good." For those shy about using something even remotely resembling a swear word, there's always "hecka," although it lacks the same impact.

What it used to mean – A Norse goddess whose task is to decide the fates of everyone who dies of old age or sickness.

Hidden agenda (n.)

Who uses it – Conspiracy theorists and political activists who are sure the other side is trying to sneak something by them, the second category being a significant subset of the first. Shallow people who believe in the deep state.

What it means – Ulterior motive.

What it sounds like – The committee chairman took the agenda from the podium and locked it away where no one could find it because he was paranoid someone might realize he wasn't following it once he called the meeting to order.

High ceiling (n.)

Who uses it – Sports analysts. Not hobbits, gnomes or Lilliputians.

What it means – Great potential. Applied to a young prospect who could wind up being an all-star or even an all-time great.

What it used to mean – A ceiling more than eight feet high. For example, a vaulted ceiling, which has nothing to do with the pole vault and which would therefore never be referred to by sports analysts.

Hindsight's 20-20 (decl.)

Who uses it – Analysts who want to point out the shortcomings of other analysts.

What it means – It's a lot easier to explain something after the fact than to predict it.

What it sounds like – "I don't want to hear what you have to say. I could have figured that out myself." Something you might hear from an optometrist, or from a fan of *60 Minutes* while criticizing a competing TV newsmagazine.

Hive mind (n.)

Who uses it – People, often online, seeking suggestions or recommendations.

What it means – "I'm stumped. I can't come up with any good ideas. Help! I'm dying here!"

What it sounds like – "I'm wish I were a bee. Bees are, like, so much smarter than humans and know everything about the world because they work together all the time. Plus they make honey. I like honey! Oh, *please*, can't I be a bee?"

What it also sounds like – An overused trope in science fiction: Introduce a seemingly invincible alien race, then resolve your conflict by making the hero defeat one part of the hive mind, thereby short-circuiting the entire collective with a single act. See: *The Best of Both Worlds* (*Star Trek: The Next Generation*), *Independence Day*, etc.

Ho (n.)

Who uses it – People with far less class than the person they're trying to denigrate.

What it means – Something so crude and offensive I'll leave it to you to look it up in a real dictionary.

What it used to mean – Santa got cut off before he could get to "Merry Christmas!" A yard tool, without the "e." A kind of model train that's bigger than N-Gauge but smaller than Lionel. The last name of a Hawai'ian singer named Don or a character on *Hawaii Five-O* named Chin, portrayed by Kam Fong in the original series and Daniel Dae Kim in the reboot.

Honestly (adv.)

Who uses it – Too many people, usually verbally and seldom in writing.

What it means – A placeholder to start a sentence and make sure your listener is paying attention. Occasionally also used as a means of emphasizing the veracity of something you're about to say. Other options used with similar frequency include "actually," "really" and "seriously." Less common, but just as annoying: "To tell the truth."

What it sounds like – Someone protesting too much. Did you think I expected to you start your sentence with, "dishonestly" or "ignore everything I'm about to say because I'm going to try to pull the wool over your eyes"?

Hot take (n.)

Who uses it – Sports commentators who like to pretend their opinion will remain relevant longer than something you take home in a doggie bag. It won't.

What it means – A take (opinion) that isn't cold.

What it sounds like – What happens when a film crew shoots a scene in Death Valley.

Hotly contested (adj.)

Who uses it – Sports announcers (occasionally, in describing something like a pennant race), political analysts (almost inevitably, on election night and near-countless days leading up to it).

What it means – Politically speaking, candidates, their parties and political action committees are dumping millions of dollars into TV ads nobody likes, mailers nobody reads and public appearances attended only by people who would have voted for them anyway. This money might be better spent on funding the initiatives they're vowing to be fight for if they get elected. But they don't care. All they care about is getting into office and kicking back amid all the gridlock the popularity contest they're paying for helped to create.

What it sounds like – A fight between dragons.

I could care less (decl.)

Who uses it – People who couldn't care less but say they could because they don't know any better. To quote Inigo Montoya from *The Princess Bride*, "I do not think it means what you think it means."

What it means – "I couldn't care less," which means the exact opposite but is really what they're trying to say. Often used immediately following "meh" or "whatever" to drive home the depth of one's apathy.

What it sounds like – You care a lot. A whole lot. You just don't want to admit it.

Impact (v.)

Who uses it – People who don't know whether to use "affect" or "effect." They're looking for a verb, but instead of consulting a dictionary, why not choose a word that's spelled the same as both a noun *and* a verb? It's so much easier that way! (Sorry, but I'm not going to let you off the hook on the affect/effect question. Look it up yourself.)

What it means – "I'm too lazy to use a dictionary. Even an online one."

What it used to mean – One of your molars has been blocked from breaking through the gum, making a visit to the dentist necessary.

In a nutshell (prep.)

Who uses it – Someone who thinks her time is too important to be wasted on a detailed explanation. Or someone trying avoid being exposed as ignorant by fumbling around for information he doesn't have.

What it means – A condensed version of the facts.

What it used to mean – Where a nut resides. Not the human kind, but the kind that comes in handy for fuzzy-tailed rodents in the habit of storing up food for the winter. These animals may not be nuts themselves, but they are a little squirrely.

In the ballpark (prep.)

Who uses it – Teachers and bosses. The same people who liked to be on the hiding end of hide-and-seek, and who loved taunting fellow players with "you're getting warmer" and "you're almost there!"

What it means – "You've got the right idea. Basically. But you're too stupid to say it the way I'm going to explain it to you. That's why I'm the boss."

What it used to mean – At Dodger Stadium or Fenway Park or Wrigley Field.

In the pipeline (prep.)

Who uses it – Bureaucrats who want to justify delaying something by days or weeks that should have taken hours.

What it means – In transit; on its way. Kind of like saying, "the check's in the mail." The implication: "Pipelines get clogged, so hey, it's not my fault if it got stuck somewhere after I got done with it. It's your problem now."

What it sounds like – A clogged sewer. I won't get any more specific than that. You're welcome.

In the wake of (prep.)

Who uses it – Wordy writers.

What it means – After. But saying a single five-letter word doesn't sound impressive enough, so you draw it out. First you try "following," but that's still just one word, so you go for something even more pompous sounding. Maybe you try "on the heels of" or "in the aftermath of," but more likely you'll settle on this one because you've heard it the most.

What it used to mean – A disturbance in the water created behind a ship as it moves from one place to another. Not to be confused with "at the wake of," which deals with attending a social gathering to mark the passing of a loved one, where people tend to get drunk and make crude jokes ... at least in the movies. (A sanitized version of this is may be referred to as a celebration of life, even though the person is quite dead and celebrating might seem be a little bit callous, given the circumstances.)

Incentivize (v.)

Who uses it – Reincarnated sadists who, in their former lives, would have been experts at using thumbscrews, the rack or a cattle prod to provoke a desired response: usually a confession to some crime they didn't commit. These days, such heartless souls are often found in corporate offices, coming up with ways to "incentivize" their employees to do more work for less money. Others spend their time advocating for the use of waterboarding against foreign prisoners accused of various crimes.

What it means – Make someone want something they wouldn't ordinarily want by making it appear more attractive, more effective or more prestigious than it really is. Offer a $10 Starbucks card to the first person who can cram 30 hours' worth of work into 20. Then tell the other employees, "See? She can do it. You can do it, too. And if you don't, you know more cuts are just around the corner."

What it sounds like – What Def Leppard might have named the follow-up to its album *Adrenalize*, if they hadn't called it *Slang* instead. Which is what "incentivize" is: corporate slang.

Inside the Beltway (prep.)

Who uses it – Cable news commentators who point out how clueless politicians are because they spend so much time in Washington, D.C. – even though the commentators spend most of their time there, too.

What it means – A reference to something that only makes sense to people in D.C., but has no relevance in the real world.

What it sounds like – Something got stuck in your vacuum cleaner.

Interface (v.)

Who uses it – Businesspeople for whom even "take a meeting" isn't pretentious enough.

What it means – To meet or confer. In this context, it has nothing to do with computers, whose operations are far more sophisticated and productive than what goes on when people interface during a business setting.

What it sounds like – Something the Geek Squad does. A noun masquerading as a verb.

It is what it is (decl.)

Who uses it – Fatalists who tell you to accept things the way they are and quit grousing about whatever's been bothering you, whether it be the wage gap, racial inequality or the fact that your favorite online site changed its algorithm so no one sees your posts anymore, despite your diligent attempts to use the most meaningful hashtags.

What it means – "I know you're pissed as hell about this and want to scream, but you don't want to look like a whiny baby, do you? You'd be better off just shrugging your shoulders, repeating this meaningless mantra, and pretending it doesn't matter."

What it used to mean – It never meant anything. You might as well say, "My car is a car."

It's the journey (decl.)

Who uses it – Someone trying to make you feel better about your lack of progress in meeting a goal or fulfilling a dream. (It usually comes off sounding like a preachy mix of denial and sour grapes.) The same people who award participation trophies to utter failures.

What it means – "You haven't achieved what you set out to do, but that was never important anyway. What's important is that you learned something along the way." How this is often received by people wrestling with major disappointments: "That was a lousy idea in the first place, and you're a total loser, but don't worry about that. It was never important anyway ... and neither are you!"

What it used to mean – "Turn right at the stop sign and keep going until you hit the grammar school, then hang a left for three blocks and ..."

Jihad (n.)

Who uses it – It's an Arabic word associated with Islam, but you probably learned it from politicians running for re-election or TV journalists trying to jack up their ratings. Why? Because fear sells.

What it means – Within Islam, it means, "struggle," especially a noble struggle for personal righteousness and a better society. Since the September 11, 2001 attacks by Muslim fanatics on the East Coast, it has been used ad nauseam in a narrow sense to mean "violent holy war."

What it sounds like – Whether used by radical Muslims or American politicians: a scare tactic.

Jump the shark (v.)

Who uses it – Critics who think any phrase with the word "shark" in it automatically sounds way cooler. You know, like shark attack, shark tank, sharknado ...

What it means – Past its prime. The phrase originally referred to an episode of the sitcom *Happy Days*, during which a character named Fonzie put on water skis and jumped over a shark. It was believed to be the point at which the show's quality began to decline. Because this happened more than four decades ago, many people who use the term probably never saw a single episode of *Happy Days*, either before or after the show "jumped the shark." As a side note, however, Henry Winkler – who played Fonzie – finally won a primetime Emmy award (for a different role) 41 years after the episode aired.

What it sounds like – An outtake from *Jaws*, the blockbuster film from two years earlier.

Just sayin' (decl.)

Who uses it – Social media users who feel the need add a touch of sarcasm at the end of a statement, while pretending to soften the blow (aka false humility).

What it means – "I just got finished sharing my opinion, which is obviously the right one, but I'm going to pretend to be gracious and admit that someone else might think differently. Which is perfectly OK. Even though they'd be wrong." It's bad enough that these two words add nothing of substance to a statement. Even worse: using the present tense to describe something that's already happened. Since this phrase is always used at the end of a statement, it would be correct to write, "Just said" – but that sounds even sillier.

What it sounds like – You're being disingenuous.

Karma (n.)

Who uses it – New Age folks trying to show off their Hindu chops. John Lennon, who found it sold more records than "instant coffee," "instant breakfast" or the difficult-to-rhyme "instant gratification." (Imagine that!)

What it means – "I'm pissed that someone did something mean to me, but the universe will take vengeance on them! I really believe that. (Even though I don't believe in a vengeful Judeo-Christian god. That's different.)" In other words, the universe has created a cosmic voodoo doll of your enemy and is poised to poke needles in it at this very moment. Some people say karma is "a bitch," but there's no evidence to support it ever having taken the form of a female dog. It's related to the term, "what comes around goes around," which works better when applied to a merry-go-round, a spinning top or a vinyl record. If bad things didn't happen to good people, and vice versa, this idea would seem a lot more credible.

What it sounds like – Dharma, which is a different, Buddhist concept that means something like "cosmic order." It's also the name of a character played by Jenna Elfman in an old sitcom, as well as the stage name of Donald Bruce Roeser (Buck Dharma), guitarist for Blue Öyster Cult. The band's biggest hit, incidentally, was *Don't Fear the Reaper*, which might indicate that karma in the next life isn't as big a worry we've been led to believe.

Kick the can down the road

(v.)

Who uses it – Political analysts commenting on the gridlock in Washington. It's a poor analogy, though. To picture D.C. gridlock, imagine a can embedded in newly poured asphalt that won't move even if it's dynamited, pulled by a 20-mule team and pushed by a front loader, all in rapid succession.

What it means – Avoid making an important major decision, often by doing something incremental instead or by waiting for someone else to figure it out.

What it used to mean – Striking a tin or aluminum can with one's foot while walking down the street.

Killer instinct (n.)

Who uses it – Sports announcers, especially boxing announcers. Mike Tyson had it. Floyd Mayweather didn't.

What it means – Once you're ahead in a game or have the other fighter hurt, you apply more pressure in an attempt to eliminate any threat from your competitor.

What it used to mean – Something a lion has in relation to a gazelle, or a housecat has in relation to kibble.

Laser-focused (adj.)

Who uses it – People trying to distract others from the fact that they, themselves, are easily distracted.

What it means – Engaged. Attentive. Concentrating. But people don't use these terms as much because terms like "laser-focused" and "dialed in" sound so much trendier and more contemporary. Never mind that lasers have been around since 1960 and that dials on telephones and TVs are relics of the last millennium. No one dials in on anything, anymore, but none of that matters in the nonsensical world of clichés, catchphrases and motivational spewing.

What it sounds like – The hypervigilant state of a cat determined to catch the point of light projected by a laser pen. It's a futile task, just like the task of persuading people to stop using this silly phrase.

Legit (adj.)

Who uses it – People trying to sound hip by shortening the word "legitimate" to two syllables.

What it means – Valid. Legitimate.

What it sounds like – Part of the title of an old M.C. Hammer release. If you hear this truncated term too often, it may make you ill – as in ill-legit(imate).

Limited time only (n., adj.)

Who uses it – The same salespeople who charge twice as much for a product than it's worth, then "mark it down" to fifty percent above wholesale and pronounce it the deal of the century.

What it means – "We couldn't sell any of this shit,

so we're trying to get rid of it by selling it to idiots who don't know how useless it is. If that doesn't work, we'll toss it in the Dumpster out back." Used whenever a company's products aren't very good or its prices are too high. Otherwise, this stuff would have sold in the first place.

What it used to mean – The same thing. Sales tactics haven't changed much.

Literally (adj.)

Who uses it – Illiterates.

What it means – "This is really important, and I *know* I'm right about it, so I'll throw in this extra word to make sure you believe it." Also: a synonym for "uh" and "like" and a number of other verbal placeholders that mean, "I can't think of the right word, but I don't want to pause for fear that *you'll* take it as a cue to say something meaningful instead."

What it used to mean – Adverb applying to something that's true or has happened. It only has any meaning in contrast to "figuratively," which signifies that something's not true or hasn't happened; you're just trying to illustrate a point. Note how no one ever says anything like, "I'm figuratively going to bust a gut" (even though that's what they mean).

Litmus test (n.)

Who uses it – Political critics who want to make their opponents seem closed-minded about some issues, often while they themselves are closed-minded about others.

What it means – What true believers use to weed out independent thinkers by staking out rigid positions. Used increasingly among partisans as a way to make themselves less relevant to more people who actually have brains in their heads and refuse to "get with the program."

What it used to mean – The use of litmus paper to measure alkaline levels.

What it sounds like – Politically active residents of suburbia are getting increasingly fanatical about the chemicals in their swimming pools.

Low-hanging fruit (n.)

Who uses it – Political analysts hard up for an original allegory.

What it means – An easy target.

What it used to mean – Fruit. On a tree. That's relatively low to the ground. Related to the similarly arboreal "easy pickings" and "slim pickings," not to be confused with Slim Pickens, an actor and rodeo rider whose birth name was the much less colorful Louis Burton Lindley Jr.

Lurker (n.)

Who uses it – Social media users.

What it means – That annoying person who joins a group but never comments and participates in any way. Might be a harmless observer or the online equivalent of a peeping tom. A stalker without the evil intent.

What it sounds like – Berserker, those Norse warriors who went into a trance before launching a frenzied assault on their enemies. Lurkers who become berserkers are the worst kind.

Mansplain (v.)

Who uses it – Writers who want to sound trendy and socially significant, especially those seeking to bolster their sensitivity credentials with the political left.

What it means – What happens when a man speaks condescendingly to a woman, especially about a subject she knows as well or better than he does. Somehow, the words "condescend" or "being an asshole" just didn't cut it, so this new one was coined. But that was only the beginning. Just as Watergate spawned a whole host of contrived words with -gate suffixes, "mansplain" has given rise to a similar bevy of unoriginal knockoffs. There's "whitesplain" and "womansplain" and even "Damonsplain," which is peculiar to actor Matt Damon. Can someone please explain to me why we need so damn many ways to explain the wrong way to explain things?

What it sounds like – A bland variety of sandwich spread. Man, it's plain!

Man up (v.)

Who uses it – Sexist Neanderthals.

What it means – Injunction with roughly the same meaning as "grow a pair."

What it sounds like – Almost as offensive as "grow a pair."

Manicured (adj.)

Who uses it – Golf announcers, when referring to greens and fairways, and journalists in general when writing about cut grass.

What it means – Recently, evenly and expertly mowed.

What it used to mean – Something done to fingernails and a beauty parlor. Pedicures are often done at such establishments, too, but for some reason, grass is never referred to as well-pedicured.

Mashup (n.)

Who uses it – The same people who think "sampling" other musicians' tunes is, in some universe, original.

What it means – A combination of two musical pieces that sounds innovative even though there's nothing original about it. (No relation to the old TV show set in a mobile army surgical hospital during the Korean War.)

What it used to mean – A potato casserole.

Maximize efficiencies (v.)

Who uses it – A boss who's about to fire you.

What it means – "You're going to have to work harder for less money so we don't have to lay you off. Also, ignore the state law that says you get two 15-minute breaks every four hours ... but if you ever tell anyone we said that, we *will* lay you off." Six months later: "Sorry, that didn't work. We've got to lay you off anyway."

What it used to mean – Buying energy-saving lightbulbs and turning the air conditioner to 73 instead of 72.

Meh (intj.)

Who uses it – People who combine apathy and laziness, taking both to new heights.

What it means – "I don't care enough about what you're saying to utter more than a single syllable, which makes me sound like I'm talking in my sleep."

What it sounds like – A muffled burp. Half a meow from a cat that's just as lazy as you are.

Men! (intj.)

Who uses it – Women who want to express their frustration with every single member of the opposite sex because one guy was an asshole or dared to disagree with them. (Before you judge me for being too harsh, please see my entry on <u>women!</u> I'm an equal-opportunity author when it comes to dishing out sarcasm. This entry just happened to come first, alphabetically.)

What it means – "My boyfriend is entirely clueless."

What it sounds like – Misandry. Which does seem to love company.

Mitigate (v.)

Who uses it – Lawyers, who usually lengthen it (as they are prone to do with just about everything) into the phrase "mitigating factors."

What it means – "My client isn't really guilty because he's such a good guy. He got straight-A's in college, doesn't use methamphetamine and goes to bed before midnight unless his favorite infomercial happens to be on."

What it sounds like – A controversy that might arise from a first baseman using an illegal mitt.

Money-back guarantee (n.)

Who uses it – Advertisers who want you to buy something that it's almost impossible to return or agree to a deal that's almost impossible to cancel.

What it means – "Just try to get your money back. We can all but guarantee that you won't have the patience to jump through all the hoops necessary to do so – you know: reams of paperwork, a thirty-day waiting period, an FBI background check, that sort of thing."

What it sounds like – A con job.

Move the needle (v.)

Who uses it – Pollsters and the journalists who worship them.

What it means – To create measurable change, based on causing a needle on a measuring device (sound system seismograph, heartbeat monitor, etc.) to move.

What it used to mean – What a person did when the phonograph began to skip at a certain damaged place on a record. You had to "move the needle" to get the song playing again. But most people don't remember this.

What it used to mean, too – Something a nurse was forced to do after being unable to find a vein from which to extract blood, despite having already stabbed you repeatedly in various locations.

Namaste (intj.)

Who uses it – The same people who use "karma" (not necessarily including John Lennon or his fans).

What it means – Literally, "I bow to you," or more colloquially, "The divine in me recognizes the divine in you." It's hard to make fun of a word with such a noble purpose, except that it's used entirely too much in a society that raises serious questions about whether there's really *that* much divinity floating around out there. When it comes to ubiquitous use, "namaste" is to New Age circles what "amen" is to American Protestantism.

What it sounds like – "Nasty" with an extra syllable, albeit the last syllable sounds like "ay" rather than a long "e."

Nastygram (n.)

Who uses it – An internet junkie who wants to sound sarcastic and technologically savvy at the same time, but is neither.

What it means – A purposely offensive email.

What it sounds like – A moldy graham cracker. A lightweight bit of nastiness (weighing approximately one gram).

New and improved (adj.)

Who uses it – Advertisers who want you to forget just how bad the original product was.

What it means – "We got it wrong the first time, but please give us another chance. We've added half a dozen new ingredients that don't do anything except make it smell better and give us an excuse to jack up the price. Even so, buying our product will help you get more dates, impress your neighbors and increase your chances of getting a promotion. (We can't guarantee any of that, and it hasn't been scientifically tested, but we'll only tell you that in the fine print that nobody reads.)"

What it sounds like – "There's a sucker born every minute."

New normal (n.)

Who uses it – The same people who declare that it is what it is.

What it means – Things used to be like that. Now they're like this. Get used to it, because it ain't gonna change.

What it sounds like – "I'm a pompous ass who can predict the future. If you have any hope that things are going to get better, it's only because you're naïve. Stop whining and accept your fate like a good little drone."

Nirvana (n.)

Who uses it – Fans of Eastern spirituality who prefer it to the concept of heaven, presumably because they don't like trumpet music (sorry, Louis Armstrong), streets of gold (too capitalist) and pearly gates (also too capitalist because they appear to have been named after Microsoft's smiling founder).

What it means – The ultimate goal for Buddhists, which means "blowing out" (like a candle, not like breaking wind) or "quenching." Nirvana releases you from the cycle of birth, death and rebirth. In other words, it's the destination, not the journey. It was also the name of a band that achieved near legendary status before its lead singer committed suicide. That band, however, turned out *not* to be the ultimate destination for drummer Dave Grohl, who went on to found the even more successful band Foo Fighters, proving once and for all that rebirth can be a pretty damn cool thing – if nirvana doesn't throw a monkey wrench into it. (Foo fans will get that reference.)

What it sounds like – Part of the title of Robert Plant's fifth solo album after the breakup of Led Zeppelin, *Manic Nirvana*. The album reached No. 13 on the Billboard chart and produced the No. 1 mainstream rock single *Hurting Kind*, which proved rebirth was a pretty cool thing for Plant, too. And he was never in Nirvana.

Nitty gritty (n., adj.)

Who uses it – People who like rhyming. Possibly hip-hop artists and beat poets, but more likely people who eat Nutter Butters and still listen to Milli Vanilli.

What it means – The important stuff.

What it sounds like – The gunk the dentist uses when cleaning your teeth. Also: a country-rock band called the Nitty Gritty Dirt Band that had a hit with *Mr. Bojangles* in 1971. Dirt itself is gritty, which may be why the band later changed its name to simply The Dirt Band.

No 'I' in 'team' (decl.)

Who uses it – Coaches, at the direction of team owners who want to discourage players from living up to the incentive clauses in their contracts and thereby earning money that could otherwise be hoarded in the franchise's coffers.

What it means – Individual success means nothing

if the team doesn't win.

What it sounds like – Whoever came up with this saying has no faith at all in the public's ability to spell a four-letter word correctly without this gentle reminder. Perhaps with good reason. Maybe that's why it became so popular.

Noob (n.)

Who uses it – Geeks and gamers.

What it means – Newbie. What folks out west used to call a greenhorn, and what more classically educated individuals refer to as a neophyte.

What it sounds like – Boob, except with an "n".

Nothingburger (n.)

Who uses it – Politicians and TV journalists subconsciously craving a savory half-pound patty of ground sirloin with bacon, two generous slices of cheese, mouth-watering pickles, tangy onions, juicy tomatoes, fresh lettuce and delicious barbecue sauce on a sesame-seed bun ... Sorry. Got carried away there. A nothingburger has none of those things. But it also won't give you mad cow disease.

What it means – An over-hyped revelation that turns out to be nothing. Not even a burger.

What it sounds like – The fast-foot joint down the street has reduced the size of its burgers (repackaging them as "sliders") – and raised the price. Again.

Nugget (n.)

Who uses it – Journalists and fast-food restaurants (mostly those that want to serve chicken without specializing in it; like Mexican joints that serve hamburgers and hot dog stands that serve rice bowls).

What it means – For journalists, something juicy that makes a story significant – even if the rest of it is useless drivel. For fast-food restaurants, a kind of chicken that's sold for the same price as thighs and drumsticks, even though it's a much smaller portion. The upside: no bones! The downside, it's not juicy at all. On the contrary, it's usually very dry.

What it used to mean – Something only a few gold rush pioneers managed to find. A member of Denver's pro basketball franchise, which changed its team from Rockets after the team repeatedly crashed and burned. The new name didn't help much. Championships have been as rare as gold strikes in a boarded-up mine for the Nuggets, which is to say they haven't won any.

Nuts and bolts (n.)

Who uses it – White-collar analysts who think nuts come in Planters jars and bolts come flashing down out of the sky during thunderstorms.

What it means – Same thing as "nitty gritty."

What it used to mean – Usually small pieces of metal hardware that hold things. Without them, you're screwed.

Off the cuff (prep.)

Who uses it – A speaker trying to downplay the stupidity of his most recent Freudian slip.

What it means – Impromptu. Improvised.

What it sounds like – Some corporate crony attending a cocktail party has lost a gold cufflink under the table and is down on his knees hunting around for it, trying not to lose a contact lens in the process. Someone please send out a search party!

On crack (prep.)

Who uses it – People who have probably never been on crack.

What it means – The same thing as "out of your mind." But that's an insult to the mentally ill, so we don't say things like that anymore. Besides, it's not nearly as "edgy" sounding as invoking an addictive illegal drug that can rot your teeth, drain your bank account and put your life at risk. But never mind all that. It still *sounds* cool, doesn't it? Kind of like the Marlboro Man smoking tobacco looked cool until you ended up breathing through a hole in your throat.

What it sounds like – Oopsie. You just broke your mother's back!

On edge (prep.)

Who uses it – Nervous chefs with large knives. Politicians under investigation. People who owe money to loan sharks. Passengers on the titanic. Cliff divers.

What it means – Jittery, worried, nervous or anxious. A condition you don't want to have while shaving with a straight-edge razor. A no man's land between "close to the edge" and "over the edge," where the anxiety level is so high that whoever came up with this phrase omitted the definite article ("the") used in the other two phrases.

What it sounds like – You need professional help and should not be allowed in the vicinity of sharp objects.

On spec (prep.)

Who uses it – Investors who don't know what the hell they're doing but want you to think they do, so they devised this term to convince you they're doing something other than trying to pin the tail on the donkey.

What it means – On speculation.

What it sounds like – "I sat on my spectacles, and now they're broken so I can't see." Then again, no one uses "spectacles" anymore, unless they're talking about making a spectacle of themselves thanks to a bad investment on spec. Let's just hope they didn't have a lot on the line.

On the line (prep.)

Who uses it – Commentators seeking to inject a higher degree of drama into what they're describing. Usually preceded by "a lot" or "all" or "putting/laying it."

What it means – In danger of being lost. At stake (which refers to a stake in a bet, not to be confused with something you drive through a vampire's heart or a place where those accused of witchcraft were burned by ignorant zealots during the Middle Ages.)

What it sounds like – What happens when a basketball player goes to the charity stripe.

On the lookout (prep.)

Who uses it – Someone who wants you to pay attention, because you're easily distracted and might be tempted to use a simple five-letter word like "alert" instead.

What it means – Alert. Paying attention.

What it sounds like – Something's missing. How can you be on a lookout? A lookout is typically a person, so if you're standing on that person's shoulders to get a better view of the landscape, I suppose it's possible. It would make much more sense to say "on the lookout *tower*," but that would involve too many syllables and too much trouble, right? But how does that explain your hesitance to say, "alert" (while resisting the urge to add "on the" to that word, too)?

On the same page (prep.)

Who uses it – Business folks and control freaks who desperately want you to agree with them.

What it means – "Call it collaboration if it makes you feel better, snowflake, but you'd damn well better do it my way."

What it sounds like – Two people fighting over an instruction manual. This never happens. Or over a rare edition of an X-Men issue. This probably happens more than you'd think.

Open-door policy (n.)

Who uses it – Bosses who want to appear transparent, whether they really are or not.

What it means – You can approach me about any concern at any time. Unless I'm in a meeting. Or on vacation. Or you have a complaint. Or I'm in my office watching the Super Bowl with the door closed.

What it sounds like – "It's too hot and stuffy in here. I need some circulation to let out all the hot air that built up while I screamed at my employees about being such idiots. Behind closed doors, of course."

Opposites attract (decl.)

Who uses it – People who want to defend being attracted to someone their parents wouldn't approve of, without admitting that their parents might just know something about the subject.

What it means – "Don't worry if you have absolutely nothing in common with your partner. You're not supposed to!"

What it sounds like – A recipe for a lousy relationship.

Optics (n.)

Who uses it – Those searching for a polite way of saying that the truth is ugly, so we should avoid looking at it, whatever the cost.

What it means – How something appears, regardless of whether it has any merit. Aesthetics. Style before substance. Political expedience. And so on and so forth.

What it sounds like – A pair of glasses that's worn as a bad disguise because you're afraid of touching a nerve (the optic nerve, naturally).

Organic (adj.)

Who uses it – The same marketers who tout "gluten-free" food as a miracle cure-all.

What it means – Healthy or grown without preservatives; arising naturally – however you define that.

What it used to mean – The term "organic" has historically applied to living organisms or material taken from them, yet people still talk about "organic vegetables." What's the alternative? Organic rocks? No such thing. No one would refer to "inorganic granite" because it's inorganic by definition. But don't tell that to the people who market health food. They use the term "organic" the same way detergent companies use "new and improved" – to signify that their product is somehow better than what the other guy is selling. Inorganic stuff like marbles and thumbtacks and Tupperware. You know, all those really tasty alternatives. But if the marketing department at the health food company says it, it must be true, right? Just remember: Cigarettes were once marketed as a way to sooth a sore throat and even lose weight. We all know how that turned out. And they're made from organic material, too!

Outside the box (prep.)

Who uses it – Business leaders who demand that workers seek new ways of doing things because they have no original ideas of their own (but who don't want to go by the book, because they already know that doesn't work).

What it means – A different perspective.

What it sounds like – Where a cat spends the minority of its time. Unless it's Schrödinger's cat, which is never outside the box but which is supposedly alive and dead at the same time – an assertion that's about as silly and tiresome as the phrase presented here.

PC (adj.)

Who uses it – People who want you to conform to a certain style of speech in the belief that doing so confers a greater degree of respect upon a particular population. Also, people who resent being told to conform in this manner because they believe that those in the first group are trying to restrict their freedom of speech. Or trying to get them to respect people they don't respect. Or trying to keep them from being bigots. Or all of the above.

What it means – An argument. Guaranteed.

What it used to mean – A personal computer. You know, the thing you used to type on at your desk before you used that eensie-weensie, itty-bitty keyboard on your phone to text abbreviations like LOL and BRB. ICYMI.

What it sounds like – Peacey. But it's more warry.

Panties in a wad (n.)

Who uses it – Friends who think you're overreacting but who want to say something more colorful than simply telling you to "chill." People with an unnatural interest in the state of your undergarments.

What it means – Preceded by "don't get your," it's used to indicate someone thinks you're overreacting to a simple problem that could be easily solved if you just wouldn't make such a big deal about it. Variants: Undies in a bundle, knickers in a knot.

What it sounds like – The washing machine broke, and this is the result.

Paradigm shift (n.)

Who uses it – Anyone who wants to sound impressive.

What it means – A change in the way you look at things.

What it sounds like – The title to a science fiction novel. "The Andromeda Strain." "The Martian Chronicles." And now, "The Paradigm Shift"!

Perfect storm (n.)

Who uses it – Someone making excuses.

What it means – A conjunction of unlikely events that results in the worst of all possible outcomes.

What it used to mean – A rainstorm that arrives during a drought, at the last possible moment before all the crops are going to die, which would be the best of all possible outcomes. Funny how the meaning got turned around here. Almost Orwellian.

Persons (n.)

Who uses it – Prosecutors, journalists, various stuffed shirts.

What it means – The same thing as "people." People (or persons – see how weird that sounds?) only use it when they want to sound like they're being technical. Prosecutors and police refer to "persons of interest" but *never* say "people of interest." Once upon a time, there was a minor distinction between the two terms: "Persons" referred to an exact number of individuals (three persons, for instance), while "people" was used for a group of indeterminant size, such as the American people. That was before most of us were born, though.

What it sounds like – Almost as awkward and jarring as it would sound to say "childs" instead of "children."

Phone it in (v.)

Who uses it – Workers who want to seem like they're more thorough or prepared than the next guy.

What it means – Give a half-assed effort.

What it sounds like – You're using your smartphone on company time like everyone else in corporate America does. But you shouldn't be doing it to text your significant other or place a bet with your bookie on the seventh race at Pimlico.

Pick your brain (v.)

Who uses it – Business leaders who have run out of ideas and want you to provide them so they can get the credit.

What it means – Get your ideas about something.

What it sounds like – About the only other part of one's anatomy that is ever picked is the nose. Not the most endearing visual.

Play hardball (v.)

Who uses it – Analysts in referring to the politicians they cover. They want to seem "better than" those politicians, but they also revel in watching them get their hands dirty.

What it means – A willingness to play rough or dirty, to pursue winning regardless of the cost to your opponent's reputation or well-being.

What it used to mean – Playing baseball, as opposed to softball. They're basically the same, except the ball is bigger and (naturally) softer in softball, and the field is smaller. You're supposed to play fair in both sports, so there's really no practical reason why hardball should refer to one as opposed to the other. But because softball is more often played by women and baseball by men, there's an underlying message here: Hardball ain't for sissies. If you think there's a tinge of sexism to that comment, you could be right. (Chris Matthews hosts a show called *Hardball* on MSNBC. I wonder if he'll read this.)

Political theater (n.)

Who uses it – Political commentators who simultaneously disdain and crave it. "We really should be talking about the issues, but polls, juicy scandals and partisan squabbling get better ratings, so we're going to stay focused on those things."

What it means – Spinning everything to make yourself look like a messiah and the other guy seem like the devil. Pandering to the base, picking a fight with the opposition and generally making an ass of yourself to get votes and (more importantly) campaign donations. It does not refer to Ford's Theatre, where Abraham Lincoln was fatally shot by John Wilkes Booth. However, the duel in which Aaron Burr gunned down Alexander Hamilton might qualify – even though it did not take place at a theater.

What it sounds like – A poor substitute for a day at an actual theater watching a flick featuring Meryl Streep, Tom Hanks or even Paris Hilton. Well, maybe not Paris Hilton.

Post (n.)

Who uses it – Social media users, some of whom post with such passion they verge on going postal. The latter term has nothing to do with the internet, though; it stems from an unfortunate stereotype against postal workers, a few of whom took their guns to work – and used them – during a brief span of time in the late 20th century. It stuck like a stamp with super-glue adhesive.

What it means – An entry, usually short (as opposed to a blog) made on a social media website.

What it used to mean – A stick in the mud, or the cement, rising at a roughly perpendicular angle to the ground. A publication, such as the *Washington Post* or *Saturday Evening Post*, that started out being delivered by post (mail). The postal service. The word between "ex" and "facto."

Poster child (n.)

Who uses it – People who don't make posters and don't have children.

What it means – A symbol of something.

What it sounds like – The actor featured on a movie placard outside a second-run cineplex for *Home Alone* or an old Shirley Temple flick.

Potent symbol (n.)

Who uses it – Analysts of various sorts, mythographers who specialize in the study of archetypes.

What it means – Something fraught with meaning. Presumably, something that's not an impotent symbol.

What it sounds like – A phallic symbol.

POTUS (abbr., n.)

Who uses it – Journalists obsessed with using acronyms to describe almost every conceivable government agency or office.

What it means – President of the United States. Or "Please, only take us skiing."

What it sounds like – Potato. A word former vice president Dan Quayle couldn't spell, which is part of the reason he never became POTUS.

Pre-dawn raid (n.)

Who uses it – Cable news anchors. People like Anderson Cooper and Brian Williams.

What it means – A military or terrorist raid that happens in the early-morning hours.

What it sounds like – A way to catch those pesky bugs off guard with bug spray before they've gotten out of bed. Your bed.

Preventative (adj.)

Who uses it – Announcers in pharmaceutical commercials. People who, for some unfathomable reason, insist on adding an extra syllable to "preventive."

What it means – Preventive, a word that describes a step taken to prevent something from happening.

What it sounds like – A sneak peek into how the language would sound if creative people were "creatative" and sensitive people were "sensitative." Fortunately, it's not "representatative" of the direction the language is taking as a whole, but some people insist on using it just to be "argumentatative."

Privilege (n.)

Who uses it – Social activists combating institutional racism, sexism and other -isms.

What it means – People in positions of power, most commonly white cisgender males, enjoy an inherent societal advantage. This is self-evident. What isn't self-evident is that continually pointing this out will make life any better for those *without* privilege, who are the ones getting screwed.

What it sounds like – A guilt trip.

Pure speculation (n.)

Who uses it – People engaging in it while criticizing others for it.

What it means – A form of speculation that is not impure, in other words, not contaminated by such nettlesome ingredients as facts and scientific conclusions.

What it sounds like – What you engage in when you start to wonder what things, other than digestible ingredients, might be found in that hot dog or the ketchup you just slathered all over it.

Push the envelope (v.)

Who uses it – Anyone but postal workers and stationers.

What it means – Something like "push your luck." At least an envelope is a physical object that can be pushed, whereas luck can't be pushed, pulled or otherwise change its position in space – if it even exists, which is another question entirely.

What it used to mean – A phrase used in aviation to describe pushing an aircraft beyond what it was designed to do, the envelope being the supposed limit of its capabilities.

What it sounds like – Postal workers have gone on strike, and they're all refusing to deliver the mail. Instead of doing so, they're engaged in the hostile act of pushing envelopes back and forth, refusing to take responsibility for them. Kind of like the game of table football you played at your desk with a folded triangle of paper back in junior high school when the teacher wasn't looking. Or maybe you didn't. Maybe that was just me.

Pwned (v.)

Who uses it – Gamers who think it's cool to have created their own word out of a typo.

What it means – Owned, as in dominated, humiliated, destroyed and schooled by an opponent. The word supposedly arose from a tendency to accidentally hit "P" on the keyboard instead of the adjacent letter "O." Is there any real orecedent for creating a word like this? Maybe not, but think of the opsibilities! They're pverwhelming!

What it sounds like – Unpronounceable, the same way "sriracha" is unpronounceable. No marriage of incompatible consonants ever makes it past the vow(el)s.

Raft of (adj.)

Who uses it – TV journalists who like to overuse nearly archaic words to sound important, but who would only do so on the air and never in real life.

What it means – "We've got a whole bunch of something, but we're too lazy (or don't know enough) to quantify it, so we're going to go all nautical on you."

What it used to mean – A small, rudderless watercraft, often used for escape from a sinking ship.

Raise the bar (v.)

Who uses it – Employers about to demand more work for less pay.

What it means – Raise your standards (why not just say this?).

What it used to mean – Instructions given during

track and field competitions in the high jump and pole vault, or a curse uttered by tall men walking into a saloon with for the vertically challenged.

Rally the troops (v.)

Who uses it – Coaches, business leaders, politicians and just about anyone who wants to inspire otherwise unmotivated people to do something they have no desire to do.

What it means – You've done a piss-poor job of inspiring people in the first place, so now you're trying to do so again, hoping that somehow things will be different this time.

What used to mean – Provoking an armed force to advance on the enemy when anyone in his right mind knows it would make more sense to retreat.

What it sounds like – Yet another war analogy applied to situations that have nothing to do with war. Do you see a pattern here? Even when we aren't at war, we apply the words of war to our everyday, humdrum lives, having perhaps forgotten that war isn't exciting. War is hell.

Ramp up (v.)

Who uses it – Skateboarders? No, journalists. And they're a lot less fun to watch when they're doing their thing (especially when the result is a phrase as overused as this one).

What it means – Increase.

What it sounds like – Something you do when loading a moving van.

Reboot (n., v.)

Who uses it – Filmmakers, film critics.

What it means – "We can't come up with an original idea. Besides, recycling an old one will make us a lot more money from people either too young to remember the earlier version or too old and set in their ways to try something different."

What it used to mean – You got kicked in the pants. Again. Or you need to be fitted for a new pair of Doc Martens.

What it sounds like – There's nothing new under the sun anyway, so why bother trying?

Red flag (n.)

Who uses it – Those clever, clever people who believe they can see through any deception and alert the rest of the oblivious world that, hey, there's something not quite right here.

What it means – "You really shouldn't touch that burner, which I'm sure you didn't notice was bright orange and sitting right next to a stovetop dial set on 'high.' I'm telling you this because I have no faith that you're any more aware of these things than a two-year-old, because I care about you and am so much smarter than you will ever be." Not to be confused with a white flag of surrender, a checkered flag at the Indy 500 or Black Flag, the punk band (or insect spray).

What used to mean – A flag. A red one.

Results-driven (adj.)

Who uses it – The same people who use "data-driven," but this is worse.

What it means – Actions are motivated based on outcomes.

What it sounds like – Idiotic. You have to take action *before* you can have results, right? So, if you wait for results to drive your actions, you'll have a very long wait before anything happens. Whoever thought up this "principle" must not have understood how causation works. Either that, or he was counting on time travel, puppies giving birth to full-grown dogs or birds evolving into dinosaurs. More likely, he was counting on something else: employees or stockholders who just nod and go along because something sounds good. Enough of them have done so that this phrase remains popular, if meaningless.

Retrench (v.)

Who uses it – CEOs of failing businesses.

What it means – "What we're doing isn't working, so we'll have to cancel the Christmas party, close the office cafeteria, lay people off, cut salaries (except for the top executives), close stores without notice and stop honoring gift cards." Translation: We're screwed.

What it used to mean – "The enemy has broken through the front lines, so we have to fall back and try to defend a new position closer to home." Same translation: We're screwed.

Revolutionary (adj.)

Who uses it – Salesmen, infomercials, etc.

What it means – "We have a product that's just like everything else you've ever tried, but we're going to make you think it's better by calling it 'revolutionary.' Really, the only thing even remotely revolutionary about it is the new label and the deceptive new ad campaign our marketing department created to pull the wool over your eyes." The same as "new and improved."

What it used to mean – Efforts by the likes of George Washington, Ethan Allen, Oliver Cromwell, Napoleon, Robespierre, Mao Zedong, Vladimir Lenin to overthrow existing governments they viewed as oppressive. Something John Lennon (no relation to Vladimir) said he didn't want any part of in 1968.

RINOs and DINOs (acr., n.)

Who uses it – Conservative Republicans critical of people in their own party willing to compromise or work with members of the other party across the aisle. Liberal Democrats who hold the same opinion of that party's more centrist members.

What it means – Republican or Democrat in Name

Only.

What it sounds like – An extinct land mammal likely killed off by a giant meteor at the end of the Cretaceous Period, 65 million years ago. Tyrannosaurus, triceratops, etc. (DINO). A misspelled reference to a large, fierce-looking herbivore with one or two horns on its nose that's found in Africa and Southeast Asia (RINO). The black rhino is also extinct now. This is sadly appropriate, because ideological purists and "true believers" have been hunting RINOs and DINOs to the brink of extinction for the past few decades.

Robust (adj.)

Who uses it – Wine lovers who can't stop talking about their favorite vintage's "robust flavor" and insist on using the same language to talk about, say, a research paper. Probably because that paper would only be interesting to someone who'd already been through at least one bottle of wine.

What it means – Full-bodied. Brawny. Important.

What it sounds like – Something from a textbook on human origins. Such a textbook is, incidentally, bound to have an entry on Australopithecus robustus, presumably the human ancestor from whom we inherited our tendency to get drunk on wine and produce boring research papers on subjects like Australopithecus robustus.

Run it up the flagpole (v.)

Who uses it – Mid-level managers too scared to make a decision on their own without consulting the big boss.

What it means – Broach an idea to see how someone whose opinion really matters will react to it.

What it used to mean – Raising a flag. Duh. Presumably not a red flag, though. And, technically, it doesn't have to be a flag. At summer camp, it might have been a pair of underpants.

Safe space (n.)

Who uses it – Social and minority activists.

Who it's supposed to mean – A place where marginalized individuals can interact without fear of reprisals from bigoted assholes. Sounds like a good idea, right? But safe for whom? Different people are triggered by different things and have different ideas about the level of safety required, so the restrictions on free expression tend to multiply in such places. Pretty soon, you feel like you're in a three-hour TSA line at the airport waiting for clearance to say anything. Somehow, I don't think this is what was intended.

What it used to mean – A square on a chess board that was protected by another piece.

What it sounds like – There are too many asshats out there who don't respect others' rights. If they stopped behaving like asshats, we wouldn't need safe spaces.

Scalability (n.)

Who uses it – Businesses trying to justify expansion.

What it means – A term companies use to express their ability to increase production in order to meet demand.

What it used to mean – If anyone ever used it, (I doubt anyone did), it was probably in reference to a mountain and concerned how easily one could climb it. Or perhaps, in fishing, how easy it was to scale a salmon. Or, in medieval folklore, how easy it was to scale a dragon. If you could find a dragon. And if you could, I wouldn't advise trying it.

Schooled (v.)

Who uses it – Winners who like to gloat.

What it means – Taught a lesson, in public and humiliating fashion.

What it used to mean – What happened when a person received an education. And actually learned something.

Sci-fi (n.)

Who uses it – Casual fans of science fiction, which is what this means. Serious fans don't abbreviate it like this. Supposedly.

What it means – Science fiction. Arguably lightweight science fiction. "Arguably" because if you say this in a group of fans, you'll almost certainly start an argument that rivals the debate over whether fans of *Star Trek* are Trekkies or Trekkers and whether *Star Wars: The Force Awakens* was an inspired return to form or a derivative retread made worse by the needless death of a beloved character. (This is not a spoiler. The movie's been out for three years; if you haven't seen it yet, that's your problem.)

What it sounds like – The Syfy Channel, which shows sci-fi, or science fiction, or both, but refuses to identify itself using either term and has instead created the kind of deviant spelling you'd expect to see at a fast-food joint. (Drive-thru, Chick-fil-a, et. al.).

SCOTUS (abbr., n.)

Who uses it – Political reporters, usually in print rather than in verbal discourse, because, well, say it out loud and you'll get it. The same people who use "POTUS."

What it means – Supreme Court of the United States.

What it sounds like – Scrotum. A place that has balls because it grew a pair.

Sea change (n.)

Who uses it – Too many people. Journalists with an obsession for all things nautical.

What it means – Significant change or transformation. One can only wish that reporters and analysts would change their vocabulary and stop using this watered-down phrase. Maybe ditch it in the Bermuda Triangle.

What it used to mean – The same thing. The term was coined by Shakespeare in *The Tempest.*

What it sounds like – A tidal wave is approaching! Or what happens when you sail from the Black Sea into the Mediterranean.

Searing indictment (n.)

Who uses it – Journalists who might not even know what "searing" means and who would laugh if someone called it a scalding or baking indictment. (Somehow, though, a blistering indictment is acceptable; better break out a needle and some rubbing alcohol!)

What it means – "We know court proceedings are boring, so we'll make them sound more dramatic. That way, you'll watch our news reports and people will keep paying to advertise with us."

What it sounds like – "Oooh! Watch out! Don't touch that indictment! You'll get burned!" Or, "This indictment will self-destruct in five seconds."

Self-starter (n.)

Who uses it – Office supervisors, who profess to like them ... until they don't. Alternative to "go-getter."

What it means – An employee who takes the bull by the horns and gets down to work with minimal prodding or direction. Managers love them, because they don't have to waste time training or managing them and can knock off work early to hit the bar or shoot a late round of golf. But they also hate them because they know a self-starter might just be gunning for *their* job or might get them in trouble by violating company protocols in order to (gasp!) get something accomplished.

What it sounds like – One of those newfangled self-driving cars. Or a toy that animates by itself. Like a Chucky doll.

Slam dunk (n.)

Who uses it – The first person to use it was basketball announcer Chick Hearn, who coined several such terms while calling games for the L.A. Lakers. (Before that, it was simply called a "dunk shot.") If there were a hall of fame for sports clichés, Hearn would be a charter member. He's also responsible for such well-worn gems as charity stripe, air ball, triple-double and boo birds. Slam dunk may be unique in that, these days, it's used by everyone *except* basketball announcers, who now prefer the term "throw it down" – which makes some of us want to throw *up*.

What it means – Something so easy that there's no way it will turn out any other way. Automatic. Legal analysts often use it to suggest the prosecution has a strong case in the latest "trial of the century." Unfortunately, they're often wrong, because they know only slightly more about the law than they do about basketball.

What it used to mean – Something a tall or athletic basketball player does by jumping high enough to "slam" the ball down through the basket. Think this is easy or automatic? You try it. Most of the people reading this probably aren't athletic enough to touch the rim of a 10-foot basket, let alone lift a basketball above it and slam it downward toward the court. Most of the time, a slam dunk isn't a slam dunk at all.

Slippery slope (n.)

Who uses it – People who can't make a rational argument using the facts at hand, so they conjure up a hypothetical future in an attempt to discredit their opposition. The same folks who issue dire warnings about domino theories, open floodgates, snowball effects and nefarious sorts who "take a mile" once given an inch. Oddly, people still talk about snowball effects during summertime, domino theories when they're playing tiddlywinks, open floodgates during a drought and slippery slopes on the Bonneville Salt Flats.

What it means – "If we allow you to do *this*, then you'll certainly do *that*, which we cannot allow under any circumstances, even though we'd like you to think we'd allow *this*, because saying "no" would make us seem stubborn and inflexible, even though we'd really love to say "no" because we *are* stubborn and inflexible. (We just don't want anyone to know it; we have a reputation to protect, after all.)"

What it used to mean – A muddy hill. For example, the downside of that hill poor Sisyphus is condemned to ascend and descend with that awful boulder for all eternity. At least that boulder isn't a snowball. If it were, it might have a chilling effect.

Smash-mouth (adj.)

Who uses it – Football announcers with big mouths which have probably never been smashed.

What it means – The kind of football the Chicago Bears were known for playing under George Halas and Mike Ditka, aka "three yards and a cloud of dust." Not the kind normally associated with the San Francisco 49ers or New England Patriots.

What it sounds like – An alternative party pop band from the 1990s that has no connection at all with football, even less the Chicago Bears. In fact, they're from San Jose, the same city where the 49ers play their games these days. (The band did release a track called *All-Star*, but it, too, has nothing to do with football.)

Snowflake (n.)

Who uses it – Judgmental SOBs whose get a kick out of cutting other people down so they can feel better about themselves for thirty seconds ... before setting their sights on another victim. Popularized by an overstressed, delusional schizophrenic in the movie *Fight Club* whose alter ego (a soap manufacturer) picks fights for the fun of it, organizes underground blood-sport meetings and plots to blow up buildings. Now *that's* the perfect source material for profound and lasting wisdom.

What it means – An overly sensitive person who thinks he's special, everyone else is special, too, and life should hand out participation trophies.

What it sounds like – If you use this term, you might just have a massive inferiority complex and be a candidate for professional help. Especially if the name

Tyler Durden shows up mysteriously scrawled at the end of one of your journal entries. Then again, only snowflakes keep journals, right?

So mote it be (intj.)

Who uses it – Pagans, Wiccans and others who take part in earth-based spirituality.

What it means – The same thing as "amen," but without the Judeo-Christian connotations. According to the dictionary, a mote is a small particle, as in a speck of dust. Christians might recognize the word from a saying in which Jesus counsels his listeners to remove the beam from their own eyes before worrying about the mote in their neighbor's. "So mote it be," however, has nothing to do with that. In this context, it's not a noun, but an auxiliary verb meaning "may" or "might." You probably haven't heard it used that way because it's archaic, which makes it perfect for use by a belief system seeking to establish its credentials as an ancient religion.

What it sounds like – "I smote a bee!"

Sparkplug (n.)

Who uses it – Sports journalists.

What it means – The kind of athlete who provides the "spark" that gets a team going, often applied to a leadoff hitter/base-stealer in baseball or a point guard in basketball.

What it used to mean – An automotive component that delivers the electrical current needed to start an internal-combustion engine. You might want to give your car a tune-up by replacing the sparkplugs, but a tune-up start in baseball has nothing to do with a team's leadoff hitter. It occurs when a pitcher makes an exhibition or minor-league appearance in preparation for a return to the big leagues. Sorry for the confusion.

Special report (n.)

Who uses it – Journalists hyping their stories.

What it means – "An ordinary report we use to fill those rare, unfortunate moments when we can't find anything that even remotely qualifies as 'breaking news' to put on the air." At times labeled as "investigative." But often a retrospective on the anniversary of some cultural milestone or, worse, a terrible catastrophe that we're then forced to live through all over again. Sometimes referred to as a "thumbsucker," although it's doubtful many babies will be watching. Stock footage with commentary.

What it used to mean – Something really

interesting. But this was when networks only had to fill 30 minutes with their nightly news, plus maybe another hour for a weekly news magazine.

State of the art (adj., n.)

Who uses it – Salesmen, particularly in describing household appliances, televisions and other electronic equipment. More popular in the 20th century, but still heard on occasion.

What it means – "The latest! The greatest! Worth paying a lot more than its actual value so you can replace the perfectly functional model you now have. And just think! Now that we've got planned obsolescence down to a science, this one will stop being perfectly functional as soon as the warranty runs out, by which time you'll *have to* buy yet another!"

What it used to mean – A phrase often used on *The Price is Right* that would entice contestants to overbid on a piece of junk, clearing the way for another contestant to win it instead.

What it sounds like – One of the fifty states has decided to dedicate itself exclusively to art and has adopted this as its new motto. Golden State, Hoosier State, Bluegrass State ... State of the Art!

Step up to the plate (v.)

Who uses it – The usual subjects: the ones who tell people to "man up" and "grow a pair."

What it means – Have the guts to get in there and do what needs to be done.

What it used to mean – The next player in the lineup steps out of the on-deck circle and takes his turn at bat in a baseball game. There's nothing particularly gutsy about this. It's just about taking your assigned turn. Any player not willing to do so wouldn't made it onto the roster, let alone into the lineup. No particular courage is required (unless you're facing a pitcher known for throwing at hitters' heads), which makes the figurative use of the phrase silly to the point of being comical.

Stinging rebuke (n.)

Who uses it – Journalists trying to emphasize that someone just got schooled.

What it means – An effective chastisement.

What it used to mean – Something a bee does when you step on it or poison oak does when you touch it.

Stunning (adj.)

Who uses it – TV journalists, for the same reason they use "bombshell."

What it means – Used in conjunction with "development," it's another one of those excuses to keep you watching what someone considers breaking news, even though it might have been expected and may not have much practical effect. When they get tired of using this, they substitute the word "shocking," although they seldom resort to "earthshaking" or "mind-numbing." These probably have too many syllables.

What it used to mean – Someone just used a taser on you.

Subject (n.)

Who uses it – In a certain context, police and the print journalists who love to rely on their jargon when writing stories: "The subject was apprehended ..."

What it means – The speaker can't be bothered to say "person," or to distinguish whether that person is a man, woman or some other entity, like an archangel, a Martian or the creature from the Black Lagoon.

What it used to mean – The subject of a sentence

or the focus of a class in school.

Synergize (v.)

Who uses it – Businesses and motivational speakers.

What it means – Work together, specifically by combining two elements to create something that's "more than the sum of its parts" (a phrase that is, likewise, overused).

What it sounds like – The transporter operator on *Star Trek* flubbed a line when he meant to say, "Energize!"

Take a meeting (v.)

Who uses it – Supervisors and ambitious clones who want to make a meeting appear weightier than it is, as though something might actually get done this time. We all know, however, that won't be the case. Most workers would rather say, "Yeah, take this meeting and shove it."

What it means – Meet. One syllable is all that's necessary here, but extending words is what business types do to sound important.

What it sounds like – Just where are you going to take that meeting? Are you going to pick it up on the corner of Hollywood and Vine, hail a cab and let it off at Rodeo and Wilshire?

Take the bull by the horns (v.)

Who uses it – Coaches, business leaders, motivational speakers, people who know absolutely nothing about how to deal with a bull.

What it means – Confront a situation head on.

What it sounds like – A really, really stupid idea. Have you ever confronted a bull face-to-face and tried to grab its horns? I didn't think so. Because you're a lot smarter than the motivational speakers who say you should do this.

Talk to the hand (decl.)

Who uses it – A few people who like to keep using

phrases that are rapidly going out of style. This phrase was ubiquitous a few years back, but you don't hear it nearly as much these days. People are more likely to use a cruder rejoinder involving the F word, followed by "off" or "yourself." Surely this is *not* how language is supposed to evolve.

What it means – "I don't want to hear what you have to say, so I'm going to raise my hand, palm outward, toward you, so I can put an ineffectual sound barrier between us that nonetheless insults you enough to make you shut up and go away."

What people used to say – "Go jump in a lake" or "take a flying leap."

Team player (n.)

Who uses it – The same people who insist there's no "I" in "team."

What it means – Brown-noser without an original idea in his head. Opposite of a self-starter.

What it sounds like – A member of the Golden State Warriors, c. late 2010s, which explains why it sounds a whole lot more impressive than it really is: Most teams are *not* the Golden State Warriors.

The ball's in your court (decl.)

Who uses it – Lazy people who would rather sit on their asses than look for a solution.

What it means – "I hereby absolve myself of all responsibility in this matter. It's your problem now, you lucky bastard."

What it sounds like – Whoever came up with this doesn't understand sports. Basketball, tennis, volleyball and similar games involve players sharing *a single court.* There is no "your court" and "my court." There might be your *side* of the court and mine, but that doesn't roll off the tongue as well, so accuracy be damned! As tennis champ Andre Agassi once said, "Image is everything."

The $64,000 question (n.)

Who uses it – People who have no experience hosting a game show and no concept of inflation.

What it means – "How are you going to solve that problem?"

What it used to mean – The most valuable question on a game show that was broadcast in the late 1950s and became the focus of a scandal when the producers started feeding the answers to popular players.

Think of it as pro wrestling for the brain. Most people probably don't remember this, and even fewer probably recall that the show was called *The $64 Question* in its original incarnation, on radio. Sixty-four-thousand dollars isn't nearly as much money as it used to be, hardly enough incentive to risk one's reputation by cheating on national television. Then again, I could be wrong.

Theatre (n.)

Who uses it – American cinema and playhouse owners who think using the British spelling makes them sound more distinguished.

What it means – Theater. This is a nightmare for newspapers, because roughly half of such establishments spell the word one way, and the other half prefer the alternative. Since they sound the same, reporters always have to ask or look it up before committing the name of the theater/theatre to print.

What it sounds like – A marketing ploy. Sure, you have popcorn on the floor and gum under the seats. You haven't remodeled your cinema in decades and you don't show first-run movies anymore. But none of that matters because you're a *theatre*, not a theater. If you doubt this is a gimmick, please note that no one on this side of the Atlantic uses the transposed British "re" ending for other nouns, such as centre, litre, metre or fibre.

This, too, will pass (decl.)

Who uses it – Friends of despondent individuals, grieving relatives and others going through hard times. The same people who say, "It's the journey" but know that won't fly after a breakup or a death in the family.

What it means – "I have no idea what to say, and I know that nothing will make you feel better. But I feel guilty about saying nothing, so I'll say something shallow and meaningless to make *myself* feel better, even though I'm aware, on some level, that it will probably make *you* feel *worse*."

What it sounds like – A slogan used in a laxative commercial.

Thoughts and prayers (n.)

Who uses it – People who want to seem like they care about your plight but who probably won't give it another thought or remember to include it in their prayers (if they even say prayers). But it makes them sound compassionate, and don't you know it's all about optics?

What it means – "Sending thoughts and prayers because I'm a) unable to do anything about your unfortunate situation or b) too lazy or self-absorbed to bother going the least bit out of my way to actually help you. Either way, I don't want to feel guilty, and it's socially unacceptable for me not to say *something*. Don't you know it's all about me?

What it used to mean – A sincere hope and heartfelt prayer that someone's situation improves. To be fair, it sometimes still means this. But the phrase itself, always uttered in this order (it's never "prayers and thoughts") and so quick to roll off the tongue, seldom feels like anything more than a couple of nouns plugged randomly into a *Mad Libs* game during a cross-country vacation in the back of your parents' station wagon.

Thread (n.)

Who uses it – Social media users, many of whom don't know how to sew.

What it means – A post and the series of responses that follows it on a social media site.

What it used to mean – A thin strand of material guided through a needle and used to attach diverse pieces of cloth. Or, figuratively, a thread of thought, similar to a line of thinking.

Throw it down (v.)

Who uses it – Basketball announcers, ad nauseam.

What it means – What a player does when he dunks the ball. But this sounds so much cooler, doesn't it?

What it sounds like – Hype. Pure hype. Which is what too many sports announcers prefer to describing what occurs in a game.

Tightly knit (adj.)

Who uses it – People who present special reports on communities and families under siege.

What it means – Closely bonded.

What it used to mean – A quilt or tapestry in which the strands of fiber are in especially close proximity. Not to be confused with "tightly wound," which is another way of saying "on edge" – and which would refer to the strands while they're still on the loom or spool.

Tipping point (n.)

Who uses it – Analysts who like to speculate about

when, exactly, a sea change occurs but who haven't a clue about how to navigate the ocean of facts needed to figure it out.

What it means – A point in time where social norms switch directions, or a key event in producing such a change. (For example, Rosa Parks' refusal to give up her seat on the bus was a tipping point in the civil rights movement.)

What it used to mean – The point at which a milk bottle, having been bumped by the cat, begins to tip over and is sure to spill its contents onto the breakfast table. Note: Some things, like Weebles and inflatable clown-faced punching bags, do not have a tipping point.

Tired cliché (n.)

Who uses it – People who are critical of other clichés but can't be bothered to avoid this one.

What it means – A cliché that has been used so much it's no longer simply a cliché, it's a tired one. Alternately, it might be a well-worn one.

What it sounds like – A cliché on steroids or caffeine, in which case it shouldn't be tired but should be fit as a fiddle (which was once a tired cliché itself, but isn't used nearly as much as it used to be, so it should feel rested if it ever becomes popular again). If you're wondering why a fiddle should have ever been described as physically adept, the answer lies in the fact that "fit" originally meant "suitable" – as in "fit for duty." Soldiers are supposed to be fit in both senses of the word, which may be responsible for the ensuing confusion.

Too soon? (qstn.)

Who uses it – 1) Jokesters who know their joke might be in poor taste, particularly after a recent death, but want to get away with telling it anyway by expressing false remorse. 2) People who make fun of this practice.

What it means – Sorry ... no, I'm not!

What it sounds like – Similar to "with all due respect ...," except it's supposed to be funny. But, with all due respect, it's not.

Touch base (v.)

Who uses it – Corporate types seeking an excuse to waste time with yet another meeting.

What it means – "I'm a micromanaging jerk who likes to be in control of things, so I want to look over your shoulder while you're working and make sure you're doing it the proper way. That is to say, my way." Or, less pejoratively: to revisit a subject so I can determine how much progress has been made and address any concerns I have.

What it used to mean – Something a baseball player must do in order to advance and be declared "safe" at one of three slightly raised white canvas or rubber stations placed 90 feet apart in a diamond shape. A fourth station is not a bag at all, but a flat rubber marker known as a "plate." It's also not a base. No one ever speaks of "touching plate," probably because, at that point the process is complete. Or maybe because they're not hungry enough to grab a plate at the buffet. On the other hand, I could be way off-base.

Traction (n.)

Who uses it – Journalists deciding whether to update stories for the umpteenth time, even though nothing new has happened. Politicians obsessed with polls.

What it means – "People like hearing about this, so we'll keep bombarding them with the same message until they become so brainwashed they'll do whatever we want them to do."

What it used to mean – Something a good tire

provides, even during a rainstorm. What you lose when you hydroplane.

Transported (v.)

Who uses it – Journalists who transcribe, verbatim, press releases they receive from police stations, fire departments and hospitals.

What it means – Taken. The person was taken to the hospital. If she'd been transported, Captain Kirk would have said, "Beam me up!" and engineer Montgomery Scott would have complied. (Last *Star Trek* reference. I promise.)

What it sounds like – It's automatically official if someone uses this word.

Trending (adj.)

Who uses it – Internet goofballs.

What it means – Becoming popular, usually briefly and usually online. Breaking news that goes viral.

What it used to mean – Nothing. "Trend" is one of those unfortunate terms that has been cannibalized by lazy linguists who believe the solution to every gap in their vocabulary is to transform a noun into a verb, or vice versa.

People talk about impacting their environment, accessing information, journaling about their lives and headquartering their business in such-and-such a city. Something similar happened in the opposite direction to "remodel," a perfectly serviceable verb that's rudely passed off as a noun by those who couldn't be bothered to enunciate "remodeled home." If we ever manage to stop coining new words simply because we can't be bothered to learn existing ones, that will be an encouraging trend.

Trey (n.)

Who uses it – Sportscasters and sportswriters.

What it means – A three-point shot in basketball.

What it sounds like – A TV tray. But I'm dating myself: I don't think anyone uses those anymore. Or the French "tres,' meaning "very,' as in "the word 'trey' is very badly overused by basketball announcers.

Trigger warning (n.)

Who uses it – Activists worried about how a news column, painting, novel, production or other content might offend someone's delicate sensibilities. If your sensibilities are offended by the inclusion of this entry, consider yourself triggered.

What it means – Politically Incorrect Alert! Parental Advisory! Explicit Content! Call the thought police and find a bomb shelter ... er ... safe space for anyone who might be offended.

What it used to mean – Someone has a finger on the trigger of a gun, and it's pointed at your head. Duck!

Troll (n.)

Who uses it – Social media goblins, hobbitses, orcs, elves, etc.

What it means – An obnoxious jerk who says something online just to get you riled up, then keeps provoking you if you bother to respond. A stalker in training. Also: the activity that defines this person's entire reason for being. Motivations include political one-upmanship, personal insecurity, generalized bitterness, boredom and social media addiction. Typical profile: failed gamer and wannabe nerd who flunked out because he was (or thought he was) smarter than his teachers and wound up couch-surfing or hanging out at internet cafes because he couldn't find a job.

What it used to mean – A very ugly but also (fortunately) very imaginary creature from fairytales and

J.R.R. Tolkien's works. Also: the enemy of the three billy goats gruff who sought to keep them from crossing a bridge in a children's story of that title. Moral of the story: If you're gruff, the troll won't get your goat.

Turn a blind eye (v.)

Who uses it – Ironically, for the most part, people with perfect vision.

What it means – To ignore something, purposely.

What it sounds like – The action of the one-eyed Norse god Odin or a pirate with an eyepatch.

Under the radar (prep.)

Who uses it – Sneaky scoundrels, spies and politicians.

What it means – Undetectable.

What it sounds like – The position occupied by a seat cushion under the backside of actor Gary Burghoff in his role as Radar O'Reilly on *M*A*S*H*.

Under siege (prep.)

Who uses it – The same people who use embattled to describe people use this word to describe institutions. A president or a dictator is embattled, but the White House or nation is under siege.

What it means – In a shitload of trouble.

What it used to mean – In a shitload of trouble ... if you were stuck inside an impregnable fortress with limited supplies and an army outside the walls with enough time and patience to wait you out. (One might expect the army outside to be described as "over siege," but it's not.)

What it sounds like – More hyperbole from overly enthusiastic TV talking heads.

Underscore (v.)

Who uses it – Know-it-alls who want to add an air of gravitas to something that isn't all that important.

What it means – To emphasize.

What it used to mean – Something people did to identify a book title back in the Stone Age (before the proliferation of desktop computers). In the Gates-Jobs era, however, it has become customary to use the far more aesthetically pleasing option of italics. Underscoring itself is obsolete, but the word remains overused.

What it sounds like – Someone doesn't know or like the word "emphasize."

Unicorn (n.)

Who uses it – Fantasy authors, particularly Peter Beagle, who wrote about the last one. Dragons and other mythical creatures. Business experts who fancy their area of expertise just as fascinating as those mythical creatures.

What it means – A highly valued start-up company.

What it used to mean – A horse with a horn affixed to its brow, probably first identified by someone who'd had too much whisky before encountering a one-horned goat or, less likely, a narwhal.

Unique (adj.)

Who uses it – People who think that anything

they've just seen for the first time must be the only one of its kind that ever existed in this world or any other.

What it means – Something mildly different than other things, but which I think is so unbelievably fantastic that I want to set it apart by making it seem better than everything else on the planet.

What it used to mean – Something that is literally like nothing else in existence. Yes, I used the word "literally," but at least I used it correctly.

Unpack (v.)

Who uses it – Amateur psychologists who appear on TV pretending to be experts.

What it means – See "drill down." Why we should need multiple equally obnoxious terms to refer to such a simple concept escapes me. I haven't even bothered to mention "dig deeper," because I didn't want to go any further down that rabbit hole. This variation, in particular, is often used to describe the process of getting to the bottom of someone's psychological state, the implication being that the person is carrying so much "baggage" that one has to unpack it all to make any sense of what's underneath. Unfortunately, your undergarments usually wind up being strewn all over the place, and you're bound to lose a lot of socks in the process.

What it used to mean – Something you did when you returned from a very nice vacation in a very nice place. Isn't that a lot more pleasant?

URL (abbr., n.)

Who uses it – People who like to sound is if they're techies, instead of saying "web address."

What it means – How many people know that this is an abbreviation for "Uniform Resource Locator" (not the kind of uniforms worn by athletes or workers at fast-food chains)? I didn't. Some people pronounce it You-Are-El, but others say "earl," as though they were introducing British nobleman, such as the Earl of Sandwich. Hungry now?

What it sounds like – A basketball player named Monroe, also known as "The Pearl"; and actor named Holliman, who had a role on the old *Wonder Woman* TV show; a running back named Campbell who played for the old Houston Oilers; and Earl Hamner Jr., creator of *The Waltons*. Also: a chart-topping 1962 song by Gene Chandler titled *Duke of Earl*. I only mentioned that to get an earworm stuck in your head.

Utilize (v.)

Who uses it – Businesspeople who don't like the word "use."

What it means – To use something and, in the process, make it two syllables longer.

What it sounds like – What Batman does with his utility belt. What a baseball manager does when he inserts a utility player into the lineup. The word is not particularly utilitarian.

Wait for it (decl.)

Who uses it – Frustrated comedians who know that timing is everything but haven't figured out how to put that principle into practice.

What it means – "What I have to say isn't all that interesting, but I'll introduce an artificial level of suspense by saying this."

What it used to mean – An admonition made to impatient commuters at the bus stop, drivers stuck at a red light and people waiting in long lines at the supermarket check stand while the person at the register searches for their checkbook or the bar-code scanner malfunctions. Also: What you have to do if you suffer from occasional irregularity.

Wag the dog (v.)

Who uses it – Political analysts who like chasing their own tails on camera, going around in circles because they have nothing new to say. Cat people who enjoy making fun of canines.

What it means – An artificial or frivolous distraction has become the deciding factor in how to proceed regarding something far more important. The relationship between empty patriotic displays and difficult issues such as jobs, wage growth, health care and national security.

What it sounds like – If taken literally and visualized, pretty damn funny.

Walk-off (adj.)

Who uses it – Baseball announcers.

What it means – A run-scoring hit, walk or other action that ends a baseball game in the bottom of the ninth inning (or extra inning). Most commonly, but not exclusively, used as part of the phrase "walk-off home run." Just ignore the fact that players sometimes *run* off the field, or that they walk off the field after *every* inning regardless of whether the deciding run has scored. These things are irrelevant. What is important is adherence to the gospel of sports jargon, without which the language of sport would be mundane and unworthy of the awe-inspiring athletic feats it describes.

What it used to mean – What a person does before his companions say, "Bye, Felicia."

War-torn (adj.)

Who uses it – Foreign correspondents on cable networks and the nightly news.

What it means – A catch-all description typically applied to a third-world nation caught up in a regional, religious or ideological conflict, frequently as a pawn of a more powerful nation seeking to exploit its geography or resources. Interestingly, it's always torn. Never ripped, shredded, folded, spindled or mutilated.

What it sounds like – "We need to add drama to our story. This should work! 'War-torn' sounds awesomely powerful and tragic at the same time. How cool is that?"

Whatever (intj.)

Who uses it – People who want you to think they don't give a damn about what you just said or did, but who really care far more than they would ever admit because that would show weakness and betray the fact that you managed to get under their skin.

What it means – "Meh."

What it sounds like – You're protesting too much by protesting too little.

Wheelhouse (n.)

Who uses it – Business analysts and sports commentators.

What it means – Generally: a comfort zone or place where you're most likely to be effective. In baseball: that portion of the strike zone where the batter is most apt to hit a home run.

What it used to mean – An area from which a sea captain navigates and commands a ship. A massive railroad turntable that rotates so it can shift a train onto a different track.

What it sounds like – A good description of a physical place that just sounds silly when it's used in a figurative sense.

WHIP (acr., n.)

Who uses it – Stat-crazed baseball fans and announcers.

What it means – An acronym used in baseball to signify "Walks + Hits per Innings Pitched."

What it used to mean – Acronyms are problematic because they're often engineered to spell out common words, even though most of those words have nothing to do with what they're describing. Sports is particularly bad at this (see "GOAT"), thanks to analytics, which are prevalent in baseball. "ERA" used to mean a long but indeterminate period of time defined by certain events, but in baseball, it means earned-run average. A whip used to be a long leather cord used to lash people in the back. Not in baseball, where it took on a new meaning in the late 20th century and became just one of many bothersome acronyms that must be memorized if one is "serious" about the sport.

What it used to mean, too – As a verb, something that must be done before the cream sits out too long, when a problem comes along, when something's going wrong or when a good time turns around (per Devo on their 1980 album, *Freedom of Choice*).

Widdershins (n.)

Who uses it – Pagans, Wiccans and adherents of other earth-based spiritual paths.

What it means – Counterclockwise. (But why use such an odd-sounding word for counterclockwise?) See deosil.

What it sounds like – Baggy pants. A widow's shins.

Witch hunt (n.)

Who uses it – Anyone who wants to discredit or marginalize another person. Or discredit an investigation. Not to be confused with water witching, or dowsing, a practice that seeks out water, not witches.

What it means – A concerted attack on someone's character through the use of false or unproven allegations. It also assumes that being a witch is a bad thing, although you'd have a hard time persuading fans of *Bewitched* or *Charmed* or *Practical Magic* (not to mention hundreds of thousands who identify themselves as witches or practitioners of Wicca).

What it sounds like – "We've lost our witch, so we're sending out a search party."

With all due respect (decl.)

Who uses it – Science fiction and other screenwriters who think it's cool to defy authority.

What it means – Usually uttered immediately before saying something disrespectful, thereby making the entire exercise pointless and contradictory. What you're really saying is: "I'm about to disagree with you, but I don't have the guts to come right out and say I think you're an idiot because I'm afraid you might fire me or seek payback."

What it used to mean – The same thing, but in the past it was uttered less frequently, so it wasn't as obvious. I blame the writers of *Star Trek: The Next Generation* and its three spinoffs (*Deep Space 9*, *Voyager* and *Enterprise*), at least in part, for this one. This phrase was used more than 90 times in those four *Star Trek* series. I'm still a fan, but the writers are due slightly less respect for relying so heavily on this meaningless phrase. Oops, I promised no more *Star Trek* references. Sorry!

Withering criticism (n.)

Who uses it – Cable news journalists. If you hear one of them talk about a stunning development or stinging rebuke, this one can't be far behind.

What it means – The person who criticized you is very mad, and the criticism is very effective.

What it sounds like – There's an old fable about a farmer who became angry at his crops for failing to produce fruit, so he decided not to water them anymore as punishment for their insolence. They withered. Not really: There's no such fable. I made it up. But if there were such a fable, that's what this cliché would remind me of.

Woke (n.)

Who uses it – Activists who want to convey that someone is aware, usually regarding issues of entrenched societal bias and oppression.

What it means – Enlightened. Although the use of a past-tense verb as an adjective might make you wonder about the level of enlightenment concerning the English language.

What it used to mean – The past tense of the verb "to wake."

What it sounds like – Bloke, toke, joke and Coke. I'm referring to the drink, not the drug. As in, "I drank a Coke, which woke me up, but that didn't mean I was woke." (Based on this entry, you might declare the author decidedly unwoke – if that's a word – but that's OK; I need a nap, anyway.)

Women! (intj.)

Who uses it – Men who want to express their frustration with every single member of the opposite sex because some woman stood them up or dared to make them question their own manhood. Frequently followed by the declaration that "you can't live with 'em and you can't live without 'em." See also: Men!

What it means – "I can't stand this person, but I want sex."

What it sounds like – Misogyny.

YOLO (abbr., decl.)

Who uses it – People who text too much.

What it means – Acronym for "You only live once."

What it used to mean – A county in California, not to be confused with the yo-yo toy or cellist Yo-Yo Ma.

Zeitgeist (n.)

Who uses it – The same folks who use "gestalt," because they think German sounds cooler than English and more badass than Greek or Latin.

What it means – The overall cultural climate of a given time and place.

What it sounds like – Gestalt. But it's not. It means something different, but it's just as annoying and its definition is just as bland.

Zero tolerance (n.)

Who uses it – People who view the world in black and white, even though they watch their favorite shows "in living color" on a state-of-the-art 60-inch flat-panel TV.

What it means – "I'm mad as hell, and I'm not going to take it anymore. I'm sick of excuses. No exceptions. Everyone else must conform to my ideal, because I'm sick and tired of people trying to get away with shit on my watch. In other words, get the hell off my lawn!" Or, as heavyweight boxer Tony Galento once said when asked what he thought of William Shakespeare, "I'll moider da bum!"

What it sounds like – An excuse to dismiss people without considering any factors outside your narrow field of vision. Sure, you're being consistent, but is it worth the price when your head has the consistency of a concrete block?

Stephen H. Provost

The author writes about American highways, mutant superheroes, mythic archetypes and pretty much anything he wants. He spent 32 years working at daily newspapers in California as an editor, reporter and columnist. These days, he's a historian, philosopher and novelist with more than a dozen books to his credit. And he loves cats. Read his blogs and keep up with his latest activities at stephenhprovost.com.

www.ingramcontent.com/pod-product-compliance
Lightning Source LLC
Chambersburg PA
CBHW060922040426
42445CB00011B/746

* 9 7 8 1 7 3 2 0 6 3 2 9 7 *